Stand Out

Standards-Based English

Staci Lyn Sabbagh

Rob Jenkins

THOMSON

HEINLE

Australia • Canada • Mexico • Singapore • Spain • United Kingdom • United States

Stand Out 3
Standards-Based English

Staci Lyn Sabbagh and Rob Jenkins

Acquisitions Editor
Sherrise Roehr

Managing Editor
James W. Brown

Developmental Editor
Ingrid Wisniewska

Associate Developmental Editor
Sarah Barnicle

Editorial Assistant
Elizabeth Allen

Contributing Editor
Mary D'Apice

Marketing Manager
Eric Bredenberg

Director, Global ESL Training & Development
Evelyn Nelson

Production Editor
Jeff Freeland

Senior Manufacturing Coordinator
Mary Beth Hennebury

Project Manager
Carole Rollins

Compositor
TSI Graphics

Text Printer/Binder
QuebecorWorld Dubuque

Cover Printer
QuebecorWorld Dubuque

Designers
Elise Kaiser
Julia Gecha

Cover Designer
Gina Petti

Illustrators
James Edwards represented by Sheryl Beranbaum
Vilma Ortiz-Dillon
Scott MacNeill

Cover Art
Diana Ong/SuperStock

Library of Congress Catalog-in-Publication Data

Sabbagh, Staci Lyn.
    Stand out 3 : standards-based English / by Staci Lyn Sabbagh and Rob Jenkins.
        p. cm.
    Includes index.
    ISBN-13: 978-0-8384-2220-5
    ISBN-10: 0-8384-2220-9
    1. English language—Textbooks for foreign speakers. I. Title: Stand out three. II. Jenkins, Rob. III. Title.

PE1128 .S213 2002
428.2'4—dc21   2002017158

PHOTO CREDITS

Front Matter:
Page v: Courtney Sabbagh

Unit 1:
Page 5 Top: ©Geri Engberg; Bottom: Steve Raymer/CORBIS
Page 13 Left: Benelulx Press/Index Stock Imagery/PictureQuest; Right: ©Geri Engberg

Unit 2:
Page 21 Both: ©Erv Schowengerdt
Page 30: Derek Cole/Index Stock Imagery
Page 31: Thomas Hoepker/Magnum/PictureQuest
Page 32 All: ©Jean Coughlin
Page 36: Corbis Images/PictureQuest

Unit 3:
Page 48: IT Int'l/eStock Photography/PictureQuest

Unit 4:
Page 64: PhotoLink/PhotoDisc/PictureQuest

Unit 5:
Page 91: USDA
Page 95 Left: Karl Weatherly/PhotoDisc//PictureQuest; Right: ©Erv Schowengerdt

Unit 6:
Page 101 Left: Ed Edestwin/Phototake/PictureQuest; Center left: Gary Connor/PhotoEdit/PictureQuest; Center right: Stephen Frisch/Stock, Boston/PictureQuest; Right: Corbis Images
Page 103: Michael Newman/PhotoEdit
Page 104: Charles Gupton/Stock, Boston/PictureQuest
Page 116: ©Geri Engberg

Unit 7:
Page 121 Both: ©Geri Engberg
Page 132: Spencer Grant/PhotoEdit
Page 134: Barry Levy/Index Stock Imagery

Unit 8:
Page 143 Left and center: PhotoLink/PhotoDisc//PictureQuest; Right: Corbis Images/PictureQuest
Page 144 Left: Archive Photos/PictureQuest; Center left: R. Morley/PhotoLink/PhotoDisc/PictureQuest; Center right: Bettmann/CORBIS; Right: Flip Schulke/CORBIS
Page 145: Corbis Images
Page 146: ©Richard B. Levine
Page 150: James Lemass/Index Stock Imagery
Page 154: Aneal Vohra/Index Stock Imagery

TEXT CREDITS

Page 91: Nutrition pyramid from U.S. Dept. of Agriculture/U.S. Dept. of Health and Human Services
Page 92: Information on dietary guidelines from Center for Nutrition Policy and Promotion, U.S. Dept. of Agriculture
Pages 94 and 96: Information on health and fitness from Center for Nutrition Policy and Promotion, U.S. Dept. of Agriculture
Page 169: Text on Harriet Tubman adapted with permission from www.aesd.gcisa.net/sdp.school/sdpprojects/civilwar.www/tubman.html

ACKNOWLEDGMENTS

The authors and publisher would like to thank the following reviewers, consultants, and participants in focus groups:

Elizabeth Aderman
New York City Board of Education, New York, NY

Sharon Baker
Roseville Adult School, Roseville, CA

Shannon Bailey
Austin Community College, Austin, TX

Lillian Barredo
Stockton School for Adults, Stockton, CA

Linda Boice
Elk Grove Adult Education, Elk Grove, CA

Rose Cantu
John Jay High School, San Antonio, TX

Toni Chapralis
Fremont School for Adults, Sacramento, CA

Melanie Chitwood
Miami-Dade Community College, Miami, FL

Geri Creamer
Stockton School for Adults, Stockton, CA

Irene Dennis
San Antonio College, San Antonio, TX

Eileen Duffell
P.S. 64, New York, NY

Nancy Dunlap
Northside Independent School District, San Antonio, TX

Gloria Eriksson
Old Marshall Adult Education Center, Sacramento, CA

Lawrence Fish
Shorefront YM-YWHA English Language Program, Brooklyn, NY

Victoria Florit
Miami-Dade Community College, Miami, FL

Kathleen Flynn
Glendale Community College, Glendale, CA

Rhoda Gilbert
New York City Board of Education, New York, NY

Kathleen Jimenez
Miami-Dade Community College, Miami, FL

Nancy Jordan
John Jay High School Adult Education, San Antonio, TX

Renee Klosz
Lindsey Hopkins Technical Education Center, Miami, FL

David Lauter
Stockton School for Adults, Stockton, CA

Patricia Long
Old Marshall Adult Education Center, Sacramento, CA

Daniel Loos
Seattle Community College, Seattle, WA

Maria Miranda
Lindsey Hopkins Technical Education Center, Miami, FL

Karen Moore
Stockton School for Adults, Stockton, CA

Marta Pitt
Lindsey Hopkins Technical Education Center, Miami, FL

Sylvia Rambach
Stockton School for Adults, Stockton, CA

Charleen Richardson
San Antonio College, San Antonio, TX

Eric Rosenbaum
Bronx Community College, New York, NY

Laura Rowley
Old Marshall Adult Education Center, Sacramento, CA

Sr. M. B. Theresa Spittle
Stockton School for Adults, Stockton, CA

Andre Sutton
Belmont Adult School, Belmont, CA

Jennifer Swoyer
Northside Independent School District, San Antonio, TX

Claire Valier
Palm Beach County School District, West Palm Beach, FL

Stan Yarbro
La Alianza Hispana, Roxbury, MA

The authors would like to thank Joel and Rosanne for believing in us, Eric for seeing our vision, Nancy and Sherrise for going to bat for us, and Jim, Ingrid, and Sarah for making the book a reality.

Rob Jenkins

Staci Lyn Sabbagh

I love teaching. I love to see the expressions on my students' faces when the light goes on and their eyes show such sincere joy of learning. I knew the first time I stepped into an ESL classroom that this was where I needed to be and I have never questioned that resolution. I have worked in business, sales, and publishing, and I've found challenge in all, but nothing can compare to the satisfaction of reaching people in such a personal way.

Thanks to my family who have put up with late hours and early mornings, my friends at church who support me, and all the people at Santa Ana College, School of Continuing Education who believe in me and are a source of tremendous inspiration.

Ever since I can remember, I've been fascinated with other cultures and languages. I love to travel and every place I go, the first thing I want to do is meet the people, learn their language, and understand their culture. Becoming an ESL teacher was a perfect way to turn what I love to do into my profession. There's nothing more incredible than the exchange of teaching and learning from one another that goes on in an ESL classroom. And there's nothing more rewarding than helping a student succeed.

I would especially like to thank Mom, Dad, CJ, Tete, Eric, my close friends and my Santa Ana College, School of Continuing Education family. Your love and support inspired me to do something I never imagined I could. And Rob, thank you for trusting me to be part of such an amazing project.

We are lesson plan enthusiasts! We have learned that good lesson planning makes for effective teaching and, more importantly, good learning. We also believe that learning is stimulated by task-oriented activities in which students find themselves critically laboring over decisions and negotiating meaning from their own personal perspectives.

The need to write **Stand Out** came to us as we were leading a series of teacher workshops on project-based simulations designed to help students apply what they have learned. We began to teach lesson planning within our workshops in order to help teachers see how they could incorporate the activities more effectively. Even though teachers showed great interest in both the projects and planning, they often complained that lesson planning took too much time that they simply didn't have. Another obstacle was that the books available to the instructors were not conducive to planning lessons.

We decided to write our own materials by first writing lesson plans that met specific student-performance objectives. Then we developed the student pages that were needed to make the lesson plans work in the classroom. The student book only came together after the plans! Writing over 300 lesson plans has been a tremendous challenge and has helped us evaluate our own teaching and approach. It is our hope that others will discover the benefits of always following a plan in the classroom and incorporating the strategies we have included in these materials.

ABOUT THE SERIES

The **Stand Out** series is designed to facilitate *active* learning while challenging students to build a nurturing and effective learning community.

The student books are divided into eight distinct units, mirroring competency areas most useful to newcomers. These areas are outlined in CASAS assessment programs and different state model standards for adults. Each unit is then divided into eight lessons and a team project activity. Lessons are driven by performance objectives and are filled with challenging activities that progress from teacher-presented to student-centered tasks.

SUPPLEMENTAL MATERIALS

- The *Stand Out Lesson Planner* is in full color with 77 complete lesson plans, taking the instructor through each stage of a lesson from warm-up and review through application.

- The *Activity Bank CD-ROM* has an abundance of materials, some of which are customizable. Print or download and modify what you need for your particular class.

- The *Stand Out Grammar Challenge* is a workbook that gives additional grammar explanation and practice.

- The *Stand Out* ExamView® Pro *Test Bank CD-ROM* allows you to customize pre- and posttests for each unit as well as a pre- and posttest for the book.

- **The listening scripts** are found in the back of the student book and the Lesson Planner. Cassette tapes and CD-ROMs are available with focused listening activities described in the Lesson Planner.

STAND OUT LESSON PLANNER

The *Stand Out Lesson Planner* is a new and innovative approach. As many seasoned teachers know, good lesson planning can make a substantial difference in the classroom. Students continue coming to class, understanding, applying, and remembering more of what they learn. They are more confident in their learning when good lesson planning techniques are incorporated.

We have developed lesson plans that are designed to be used each day and to reduce preparation time. The planner includes:

- Standard lesson progression (Warm-up and Review, Introduction, Presentation, Practice, Evaluation, and Application)

- A creative and complete way to approach varied class lengths so that each lesson will work within a class period.

- 231 hours of classroom activities

- Time suggestions for each activity

- Pedagogical comments

- Space for teacher notes and future planning

- Identification of SCANS, EFF, and CASAS standards

USER QUESTIONS ABOUT STAND OUT

- **What are SCANS and EFF and how do they integrate into the book?**
  SCANS is the Secretary's Commission on Acquiring Necessary Skills. SCANS was developed to encourage students to prepare for the workplace. The standards developed through SCANS have been incorporated throughout the **Stand Out** student books and components.

  Stand Out addresses SCANS a little differently than other books. SCANS standards elicit effective teaching strategies by incorporating essential skills such as critical thinking and group work. We have incorporated SCANS standards in every lesson, not isolating these standards in the work unit, as is typically done.

  EFF, or **E**quipped **f**or the **F**uture, is another set of standards established to address students' roles as parents, workers, and citizens, with a vision of student literacy and lifelong learning. **Stand Out** addresses these standards and integrates them into the materials in a similar way to SCANS.

- **What about CASAS?** The federal government has mandated that states show student outcomes as a prerequisite to funding. Some states have incorporated the **C**omprehensive **A**dult **S**tudent **A**ssessment **S**ystem (CASAS) testing to standardize agency reporting. Unfortunately, since many of our students are unfamiliar with standardized testing and therefore struggle with it, adult schools need to develop lesson plans to address specific concerns. **Stand Out** was developed with careful attention to CASAS skill areas in most lessons and performance objectives.

- **Are the tasks too challenging for my students?** Students learn by doing and learn more when challenged. **Stand Out** provides tasks that encourage critical thinking in a variety of ways. The tasks in each lesson move from teacher-directed to student-centered so the learner clearly understands what's expected and is willing to "take a risk." The lessons are expected to be challenging. In this way, students learn that when they work together as a learning community, anything becomes possible. The satisfaction of accomplishing something both as an individual and as a member of a team results in greater confidence and effective learning.

- **Do I need to understand lesson planning to teach from the student book?** If you don't understand lesson planning when you start, you will when you finish! Teaching from **Stand Out** is like a course on lesson planning, especially if you use the Lesson Planner on a daily basis.

  Stand Out does *stand out* because, when we developed this series, we first established performance objectives for each lesson. Then we designed lesson plans, followed by student book pages. The introduction to each lesson varies because different objectives demand different approaches. **Stand Out's** variety of tasks makes learning more interesting for the student.

- **What are team projects?** The final lesson of each unit is a **team project.** This is often a team simulation that incorporates the objectives of the unit and provides an additional opportunity for students to actively apply what they have learned. The project allows students to produce something that represents their progress in learning. These end-of-unit projects were created with a variety of learning styles and individual skills in mind. The team projects can be skipped or simplified, but we encourage instructors to implement them, enriching the overall student experience.

- **What do you mean by a customizable Activity Bank?** Every class, student, teacher, and approach is different. Since no one textbook can meet all these differences, the *Activity Bank CD-ROM* allows you to customize **Stand Out** for your class. You can copy different activities and worksheets from the CD-ROM to your hard drive and then:

  - change items in supplemental vocabulary, grammar, and life skill activities;

  - personalize activities with student names and popular locations in your area;

  - extend every lesson with additional practice where you feel it is most needed.

- **Is this a grammar-based or a competency-based series?** This is a competency-based series, with grammar identified more clearly and more boldly than in other similar series. We believe that grammar instruction in context is extremely important. Grammar structures are frequently identified as principal lesson objectives. Students are first provided with context that incorporates the grammar, followed by an explanation and practice. At this level, we expect students to acquire language structure after hearing and reading grammar in useful contexts. For teachers who want to enhance grammar instruction, the *Activity Bank CD-ROM* and/or the *Stand Out Grammar Challenge* workbooks provide ample opportunities.

  The six competencies that drive **Stand Out** are basic communication, consumer economics, community resources, health, occupational knowledge, and lifelong learning (government and law replace lifelong learning in Books 3 and 4).

- **Are there enough activities so I don't have to supplement?** **Stand Out** stands alone in providing 231 hours of instruction and activities, even without the additional suggestions in the Lesson Planner. The Lesson Planner also shows you how to streamline lessons to provide 115 hours of classwork and still have thorough lessons if you meet less often. When supplementing with the Activity Bank CD-ROM, the ExamView Test Bank CD-ROM, and the Stand Out Grammar Challenge workbooks, you gain unlimited opportunities to extend class hours and provide activities related directly to each lesson objective. Calculate how many hours your class meets in a semester and look to **Stand Out** to address the full class experience.

  Stand Out is a comprehensive approach to adult language learning, meeting needs of students and instructors completely and effectively.

CONTENTS

EFF	SCANS (Workplace)	Academic/Math	CASAS
• Taking responsibility for learning • Reflecting and evaluating • Planning • Conveying ideas in writing	• Understanding systems • Decision making	ACADEMIC • Understand paragraph formatting • Write a paragraph • Understand educational systems • Plan educational goals	**1:** 0.1.1, 0.1.4, 0.1.6, 0.2.1, 0.2.2, 7.2.6 **2:** 0.1.4 **3:** 0.1.4, 0.2.4, 7.2.6, 7.5.6 **4:** 0.1.2 **5:** 6.7.3, 7.1.1
Most EFF skills are incorporated into this unit, with an emphasis on: • Taking responsibility for learning • Using information and communication technology • Conveying ideas in writing • Solving problems and making decisions • Planning (Technology is optional.)	Most SCANS are incorporated into this unit, with an emphasis on: • Allocating Time • Understanding systems • Applying technology to task • Responsibility • Self Management • Writing • Decision making (Technology is optional.)	ACADEMIC • Identify topic sentence, support sentences, and conclusion sentence • Work out meanings of words from context • Brainstorm ideas before writing a paragraph • Use an outline • Create a vocabulary notebook MATH • Interpret a pie chart • Estimate percentages	**1:** 0.1.2, 0.2.4, 7.1.4 **2:** 7.1.1, 7.1.2, 7.1.3 **3:** 7.1.1, 7.1.2, 7.1.3, 7.2.5, 7.2.6 **4:** 4.4.1, 7.4.3, 7.4.5, 7.4.9 **5:** 7.2.6 **6:** 7.5.1 **7:** 1.1.3, 6.7.4, 7.4.2 **R:** 7.1.4, 7.4.1, 7.5.1 **TP:** 4.8.1, 4.8.5, 4.8.6
Most EFF skills are incorporated into this unit, with an emphasis on: • Reflecting and evaluating • Learning through research • Cooperating with others • Solving problems and making decisions (Technology is optional.)	Most SCANS are incorporated into this unit, with an emphasis on: • Responsibility • Participating as a member of a team • Acquiring and evaluating information • Organizing and maintaining information • Decision making • Reasoning (Technology is optional.)	ACADEMIC • Scan text for details • Use sequencing transitions in writing • Make vocabulary flash cards MATH • Calculate prices and discounts • Compare prices and numerical data	**1:** 0.1.2, 1.3.7 **2:** 1.3.1, 1.3.2 **3:** 1.2.1, 7.4.10 **4:** 1.2.1, 1.2.2 **5:** 0.1.4 **6:** 1.2.1, 1.7.3, 3.4.1, 7.2.1 **7:** 1.2.5 **R:** 7.1.4, 7.4.1, 7.5.1 **TP:** 4.8.1, 4.8.5, 4.8.6
Most EFF skills are incorporated into this unit, with an emphasis on: • Learning through research • Reading with understanding • Conveying ideas in writing • Solving problems and making decisions (Technology is optional.)	Most SCANS are incorporated into this unit, with an emphasis on: • Allocating money • Understanding systems • Monitoring and correcting performance • Interpreting and communicating information • Reading • Writing • Decision making (Technology is optional.)	ACADEMIC • Write a business letter MATH • Use addition and subtraction to calculate totals and solve real world problems • Interpret and create a bar graph	**1:** 1.4.1, 1.4.2 **2:** 7.2.7 **3:** 1.4.3 **4:** 1.4.4, 1.5.3 **5:** 1.4.7 **6:** 1.4.5, 1.4.7 **7:** 1.5.1, 6.0.3, 6.0.4, 6.1.1, 6.1.2, 6.7.2 **R:** 7.1.4, 7.4.1, 7.5.1 **TP:** 4.8.1, 4.8.5, 4.8.6
Most EFF skills are incorporated into this unit, with an emphasis on: • Learning through research • Conveying ideas in writing • Solving problems and making decisions (Technology is optional.)	Most SCANS are incorporated into this unit, with an emphasis on: • Understanding systems • Interpreting and communicating information • Writing • Decision making • Seeing things in the mind's eye (Technology is optional.)	ACADEMIC • Use critical thinking to analyze a text and solve problems • Write a paragraph • Use context to work out meanings MATH • Interpret numerical data • Use addition to make calculations • Measure distances on a map and calculate real distances using a scale	**1:** 0.1.2 **2:** 1.8.5 **3:** 2.5.6, 6.0.3, 6.1.1, 6.1.3 **4:** 2.1.1 **5:** 2.2.1, 2.2.5 **6:** 7.2.6 **7:** 7.2.2 **R:** 7.1.4, 7.4.1, 7.5.1 **TP:** 4.8.1, 4.8.5, 4.8.6

CASAS: Numbers in bold indicate lesson numbers; **R** indicates review lesson; **TP** indicates team project.

CONTENTS

EFF	SCANS (Workplace)	Academic/Math	CASAS
Most EFF skills are incorporated into this unit, with an emphasis on: • Reflecting and evaluating • Learning through research • Reading with understanding • Speaking so others can understand (Technology is optional.)	Most SCANS are incorporated into this unit, with an emphasis on: • Understanding systems • Self-management • Acquiring and evaluating information • Interpreting and communicating information (Technology is optional.)	ACADEMIC • Predict ideas before reading • Identify main ideas in a text MATH • Interpret percentages and amounts in grams on a food label	**1:** 3.1.1 **2:** 3.1.1 **3:** 3.2.1 **4:** 3.4.2, 3.5.9 **5:** 3.5.1, 3.5.9 **6:** 3.5.3, 3.5.5, 3.5.9, 6.7.3 **7:** 3.5.9 **R:** 7.1.4, 7.4.1, 7.5.1 **TP:** 4.8.1, 4.8.5, 4.8.6
Most EFF skills are incorporated into this unit, with an emphasis on: • Speaking so others can understand • Planning • Learning through research (Technology is optional.)	Most SCANS are incorporated into this unit, with an emphasis on: • Self-esteem • Sociability • Acquiring and evaluating information • Speaking • Decision making (Technology is optional.)	ACADEMIC • Scan text for details • Use critical thinking to analyze a text and solve problems • Write a letter	**1:** 4.1.8 **2:** 4.1.9 **3:** 4.1.3 **4:** 4.1.2 **5:** 4.1.2 **6:** 4.1.5, 4.1.7 **7:** 4.1.5, 4.1.7 **R:** 7.1.4, 7.4.1, 7.5.1 **TP:** 4.8.1, 4.8.5, 4.8.6
Most EFF skills are incorporated into this unit, with an emphasis on: • Reflecting and evaluating • Cooperating with others (Technology is optional.)	Most SCANS are incorporated into this unit, with an emphasis on: • Understanding systems • Participating as a member of a team • Acquiring and evaluating information (Technology is optional.)	ACADEMIC • Use context to work out meanings of new words MATH • Interpret pay stub information • Use addition to calculate pay stub totals	**1:** 4.4.1 **2:** 7.5.1 **3:** 4.2.1, 4.4.3 **4:** 4.2.1 **5:** 4.3.3, 4.3.4, 4.5.1 **6:** 4.4.1, 4.6.1 **7:** 4.4.1, 4.6.2, 4.6.4 **R:** 7.1.4, 7.4.1, 7.5.1 **TP:** 4.8.1, 4.8.5, 4.8.6
Most EFF skills are incorporated into this unit, with an emphasis on: • Speaking so others can understand • Listening actively • Reflecting and evaluating (Technology is optional.)	Most SCANS are incorporated into this unit, with an emphasis on: • Listening • Speaking • Responsibility • Self-esteem (Technology is optional.)	ACADEMIC • Identify people and events in United States history • Predict ideas before reading • Read about government systems	**1:** 5.2.1, 5.2.4 **2:** 5.2.1 **3:** 5.1.4, 5.1.6 **4:** 5.2.1, 5.1.4 **5:** 5.5.7, 5.5.8 **6:** 5.6.1 **7:** 5.1.6 **R:** 7.1.4, 7.4.1, 7.5.1 **TP:** 4.8.1, 4.8.5, 4.8.6

CASAS: Numbers in bold indicate lesson numbers; **R** indicates review lesson; **TP** indicates team project.

Guide to Stand Out

Meeting the Standards has never been easier!

Stand Out is an easy-to-use, standards-based series for adult students that teaches the English skills necessary to be a successful worker, parent, and citizen.

- **Goals:** A roadmap of learning is provided for the student.

- **Vocabulary:** Key vocabulary is introduced, followed by interactive exercises for reinforcement.

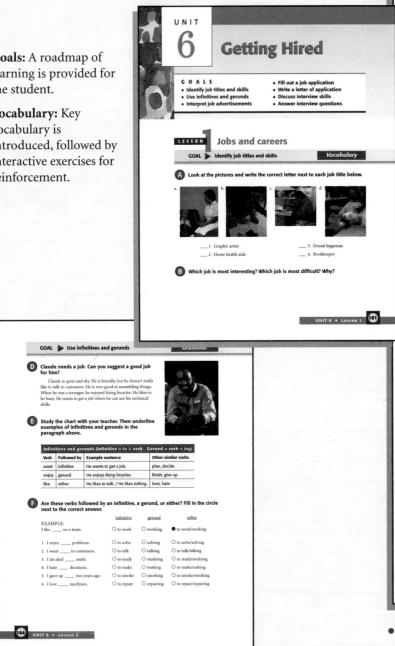

UNIT 6 — Getting Hired

GOALS
- Identify job titles and skills
- Use infinitives and gerunds
- Interpret job advertisements
- Fill out a job application
- Write a letter of application
- Discuss interview skills
- Answer interview questions

LESSON 1 — Jobs and careers

GOAL ▶ Identify job titles and skills — *Vocabulary*

A Look at the pictures and write the correct letter next to each job title below.

___ 1. Graphic artist
___ 2. Home health aide
___ 3. Dental hygienist
___ 4. Bookkeeper

B Which job is most interesting? Which job is most difficult? Why?

UNIT 6 • Lesson 1 101

GOAL ▶ Use infinitives and gerunds — *Grammar*

D Claude needs a job. Can you suggest a good job for him?

Claude is quiet and shy. He is friendly, but he doesn't really like to talk to customers. He is very good at assembling things. When he was a teenager, he enjoyed fixing bicycles. He likes to be busy. He wants to get a job where he can use his technical skills.

E Study the chart with your teacher. Then underline examples of infinitives and gerunds in the paragraph above.

Infinitives and gerunds (Infinitive = to + verb Gerund = verb + ing)		
Verb	**Followed by**	**Example sentence**	**Other similar verbs**
want	infinitive	He wants *to get* a job.	plan, decide
enjoy	gerund	He enjoys *fixing* bicycles.	finish, give up
like	either	He likes *to talk*. / He likes *talking*.	love, hate

F Are these verbs followed by an infinitive, a gerund, or either? Fill in the circle next to the correct answer.

	infinitive	gerund	either
EXAMPLE: I like ____ on a team.	○ to work	○ working	● to work/working
1. I enjoy ____ problems.	○ to solve	○ solving	○ to solve/solving
2. I want ____ to customers.	○ to talk	○ talking	○ to talk/talking
3. I decided ____ math.	○ to study	○ studying	○ to study/studying
4. I hate ____ decisions.	○ to make	○ making	○ to make/making
5. I gave up ____ two years ago.	○ to smoke	○ smoking	○ to smoke/smoking
6. I love ____ machines.	○ to repair	○ repairing	○ to repair/repairing

104 UNIT 6 • Lesson 2

- **Grammar:** Charts clearly explain grammar points, and are followed by controlled exercises leading into open-ended ones.

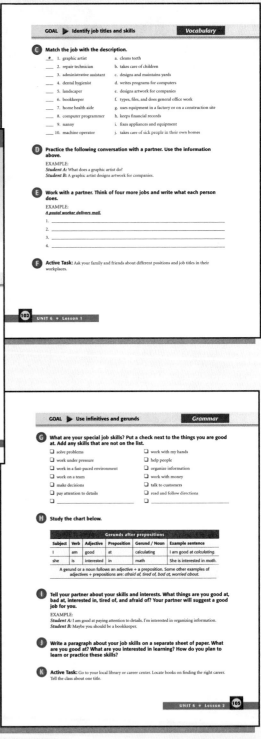

GOAL ▶ Identify job titles and skills — *Vocabulary*

C Match the job with the description.

___ 1. graphic artist   a. cleans teeth
___ 2. repair technician   b. takes care of children
___ 3. administrative assistant   c. designs and maintains yards
___ 4. dental hygienist   d. writes programs for computers
___ 5. landscaper   e. designs artwork for companies
___ 6. bookkeeper   f. types, files, and does general office work
___ 7. home health aide   g. uses equipment in a factory or on a construction site
___ 8. computer programmer   h. keeps financial records
___ 9. nanny   i. fixes appliances and equipment
___ 10. machine operator   j. takes care of sick people in their own homes

D Practice the following conversation with a partner. Use the information above.

EXAMPLE:
Student A: What does a graphic artist do?
Student B: A graphic artist designs artwork for companies.

E Work with a partner. Think of four more jobs and write what each person does.

EXAMPLE:
A postal worker delivers mail.
1. _____
2. _____
3. _____
4. _____

F Active Task: Ask your family and friends about different positions and job titles in their workplaces.

102 UNIT 6 • Lesson 1

GOAL ▶ Use infinitives and gerunds — *Grammar*

G What are your special job skills? Put a check next to the things you are good at. Add any skills that are not on the list.

❑ solve problems   ❑ work with my hands
❑ work under pressure   ❑ help people
❑ work in a fast-paced environment   ❑ organize information
❑ work on a team   ❑ work with money
❑ make decisions   ❑ talk to customers
❑ pay attention to details ❑ read and follow directions
❑ _____   ❑ _____

H Study the chart below.

Gerunds after prepositions					
Subject	**Verb**	**Adjective**	**Preposition**	**Gerund / Noun**	**Example sentence**
I	am	good	at	calculating	I am good at *calculating*.
she	is	interested	in	math	She is interested in *math*.

A gerund or a noun follows an adjective + a preposition. Some other examples of adjectives + prepositions are: *afraid of, tired of, bad at, worried about*.

I Tell your partner about your skills and interests. What things are you good at, bad at, interested in, tired of, and afraid of? Your partner will suggest a good job for you.

EXAMPLE:
Student A: I am good at paying attention to details. I'm interested in organizing information.
Student B: Maybe you should be a bookkeeper.

J Write a paragraph about your job skills on a separate sheet of paper. What are you good at? What are you interested in learning? How do you plan to learn or practice these skills?

K Active Task: Go to your local library or career center. Locate books on finding the right career. Tell the class about one title.

UNIT 6 • Lesson 2 105

- **Grammar:** Clear explanations are followed by immediate use, in this example with reading and writing.

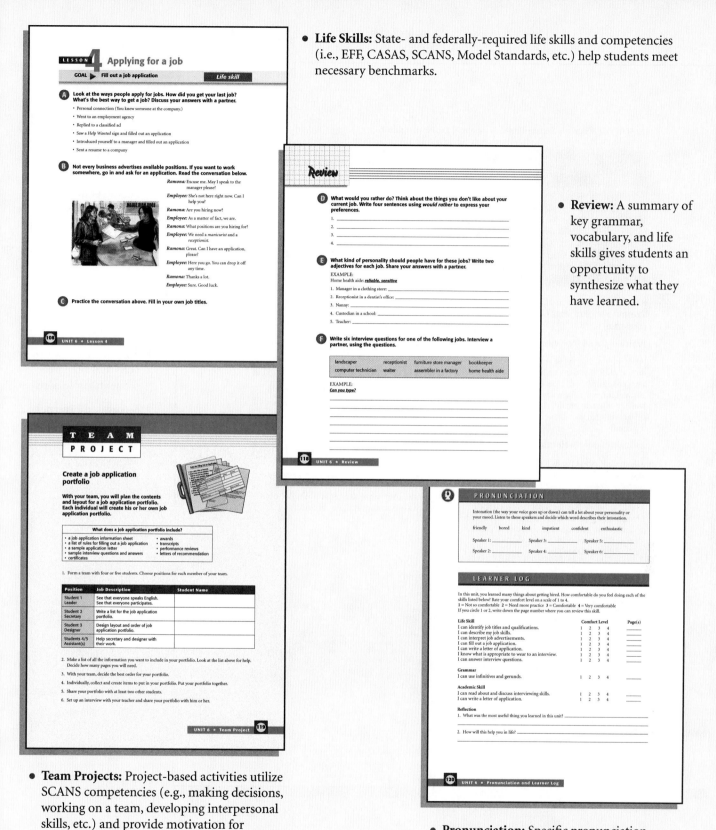

- **Life Skills:** State- and federally-required life skills and competencies (i.e., EFF, CASAS, SCANS, Model Standards, etc.) help students meet necessary benchmarks.

- **Review:** A summary of key grammar, vocabulary, and life skills gives students an opportunity to synthesize what they have learned.

- **Team Projects:** Project-based activities utilize SCANS competencies (e.g., making decisions, working on a team, developing interpersonal skills, etc.) and provide motivation for students.

- **Pronunciation:** Specific pronunciation problems are targeted and corrected.

- **Learner Log:** The final section of each unit provides opportunity for learner self-assessment.

LESSON PLAN

Objective:
Identify job titles and skills
Key vocabulary:
job, career, profession, graphic artist,
dental hygienist, home care aide,
bookkeeper, repair technician,
administrative assistant, landscaper,
computer programmer, nanny, machine
operator, homemaker, student, retired

 Pre-Assessment: Use *Stand Out* **ExamView® Pro** *Test Bank* for Unit 6. (optional)

Warm-up and Review: 10–15 min.

Write *job titles* on the board. Ask students, *What do you do?* If they don't understand the question, keep asking different students until someone answers correctly. If this doesn't work, say *I am a teacher. What do you do?* Once students start telling you what they do, write the responses on the board.

Introduction: 5–10 min.

Ask students what the difference is between a *job* and a *career*. The *Newbury House Dictionary of American English* defines a *"career"* as "a life's work, especially in business or in a profession" and a *"job"* as "work that one is paid to do every day, permanent employment." *"Profession"* is defined as "an occupation requiring an advanced degree." Discuss these terms with your students and ask them which applies to them.

State the Objectives: *In this unit you will learn what you need to do to get a job or to get a better one. For your final project, you will create a job-hunting portfolio. Today we will discuss job titles and the responsibilities that go along with each job.*

Presentation 1: 10–15 min.

Ⓐ Look at the pictures and write the correct letter next to each job title below.

Have students complete the exercise by themselves. When they are finished, go over each job as a class. See if they know what the person in each picture does before you give a fuller explanation. You might ask if they know anyone who holds a job like the ones shown. When you are finished, ask them if there are other jobs they can think of that are not listed.

Practice 1: 15–20 min.

Ⓑ Which job is most interesting? Which job is most difficult? Why?

Have students discuss the questions in groups. Ask each group to have a member take notes on the answers.

Evaluation 1: 10–15 min. 1.5+

Ask each group to report what they discussed. Write their choices and reasons on the board. See if you can come up with a consensus on which are the most interesting and most difficult jobs.

STANDARDS CORRELATIONS

CASAS: 4.1.8
SCANS: **Interpersonal** Participates as a Member of a Team, Teaches Others New Skills
Information Acquires and Evaluates Information, Organizes and Maintains Information, Interprets and Communicates Information
Systems Monitors and Corrects Performance
Basic Skills Reading, Writing, Listening, Speaking
Thinking Skills Creative Thinking, Decision Making, Reasoning

Personal Qualities Sociability
EFF: **Communication** Read with Understanding, Convey Ideas in Writing, Speak So Others Can Understand, Listen Actively
Decision Making Solve Problems and Make Decisions
Interpersonal Resolve Conflict and Negotiate, Advocate and Influence, Cooperate with Others
Lifelong Learning Reflect and Evaluate

- **Lesson Plan:** A complete lesson plan for each page in the student book is provided, using nationally-accepted curriculum design.

- **Pacing Guidelines:** Class-length icons offer three different pacing strategies.

- **CD Icon:** Supplemental activities found on the *Activity Bank CD-ROM* are noted with an icon.

- **Supplemental warm-up activities** prepare students for lessons.

- **Suggested Internet activities** expose students to technology and real world activities.

Worksheet 1 (Unit 6)

Unit 6
Worksheet 1

Name: _____
Date: _____

Job Titles

A. Read the list of job titles below. Imagine that you have the skills to do all of them. Which jobs interest you the most? (Which jobs would you like to have?) Number the jobs in order from the one you are most interested in (1) to the one you are least interested in (10) under the *interest* column.

	Interest	Ability
Administrative assistant		
Bookkeeper		
Computer programmer		
Dental hygienist		
Graphic artist		
Home health aide		
Landscaper		
Machine operator		
Nanny		
Repair technician		

B. Read the list of job titles again. Which jobs are you most qualified for? (Which jobs can you do?) Number the jobs in order, from the one you are most qualified for (1) to the one you are least qualified for (10) under the *ability* column.

C. Read about each of the employees below and write the correct job title on the line.

1. Chinh maintains financial records for a small business. She's a
_____

2. Gregory creates games for computers. He's a _____.

3. Marly cleans teeth. She's a _____.

4. Mike does maintenance in people's yards. He's a _____.

5. My mother takes care of children. She's a _____.

6. Olivia fixes washers and dryers. She's a _____.

7. Ricardo takes care of sick people in their own homes. He's a _____.

8. Rudy operates a drill on a construction site. He's a _____.

9. Satomi designs artwork for companies. She's a _____.

10. Takuji types, files and answers the phone. He's a _____.

Heinle & Heinle © 2002
Stand Out Activity Bank 3

Challenge 3 (Unit 6)

UNIT 6 **Getting Hired**

CHALLENGE 3 ▸ Adjective + preposition + gerund (or noun)

Subject	Verb	Adjective	Preposition	Gerund/Noun	
I	am	happy	about	**getting**	a new job.
She	is	good	at	**fixing**	machines.
They	are	interested	in	**computers.**	
He	is	afraid	of	**not having**	enough experience.

• A gerund or a noun follows an adjective + preposition.
• Other examples of adjective + preposition: **tired of, bad at, worried about.**
• To make the gerund negative, put **not** before the gerund.

A Complete each sentence with a gerund. Use the verbs in the box.

EXAMPLE: Claude isn't good at _____*answering*_____ math questions.

1. We are tired of _____ new workers.

2. The boss is bad at _____ the benefits program.

3. We are happy about not _____ laid off.

4. She isn't good at _____ on time.

5. Lance is afraid of _____ his job.

6. They are worried about _____ decisions.

| train |
| be |
| lose |
| answer |
| make |
| explain |
| arrive |

B Write a new sentence using *adjective + preposition + gerund*.

EXAMPLE: She writes letters very well. _*She is good at writing letters.*_

1. Learning new skills make him happy.
_____

2. He may become a landscaper. That's his strongest interest.
_____

3. She doesn't like to use electric tools. She's afraid of them.
_____

4. Ramona doesn't want to lose her job. She's worried.
_____

5. She doesn't know how to operate the machine well. She runs it badly.
_____

6. I'm tired. I don't want to explain my decisions.
_____

(margin: Adjective + preposition + gerund (or noun))

Post-Assessment Unit 6

A. Look at the job application. Then choose the best answer to each question below.

1 Name _____ Phone _____
   last   first   mi

2 Present Address _____

3 City _____ State _____ Zip _____

4 Special Skills _____

5 Type WPM _____ 6 Languages _____

7 Computer Skills _____

8 Last Five Year Employment History (Please list most recent positions first)

Employer (company, address)	Position	Dates from	to	Reason for leaving

9

	School and address	Course of Study	Number of Years Completed	Degree or Diploma
Elementary School				
High School				
College(s)				

10 REFERENCES

Name	Position	Company	Telephone

____ 1. On which part of the application will you write where you used to work?
   a. part 6   c. part 8
   b. part 9   d. part 10

____ 2. Where would you write that you speak Vietnamese?
   a. part 1   c. part 7
   b. part 4   d. part 6

____ 3. Where can you write that you have good communication skills?
   a. part 7   c. part 6
   b. part 5   d. part 4

• **Activity Bank CD-ROM:** Hours of motivating and creative reinforcement activities are provided to follow student book lessons. Instructors can download activities and add or adapt them to student needs. The audio component for listening activities will also be on CD-ROMs. Cassettes are available for instructors who prefer them.

• *Stand Out Grammar Challenge:* Optional workbook activities provide supplemental exercises for students who desire even more contextual grammar and vocabulary practice.

• *Stand Out ExamView®Pro Test Bank:* Innovative test bank CD-ROM allows for pre-and post-unit quizzes. Teachers can easily print out predetermined tests, or modify them to create their own customized (including computer-based) assessments.

Getting to Know You

GOALS

- Introduce yourself
- Greet your friends
- Use small talk
- Format a paragraph
- Discuss educational goals

LESSON 1

Meet your classmates

GOAL ▶ Introduce yourself

Life skill

A Fill out the school registration form with your personal information.

1. First Name _____ 2. Middle Initial _____

3. Last Name _____

4. Address: Number and Street _____

5. City _____ 6. State _____ 7. Zip _____

8. Home Phone _____ 9. Work Phone _____

10. E-mail Address _____

11. Date of Birth (mm/dd/yy) _____/_____/_____

12. Languages Spoken _____

13. Occupation _____

14. Hobbies and Interests _____

B Write a question for each section above on a separate sheet of paper. Then interview another student using the questions.

EXAMPLE:

Student A: What is your first name?   *Student B:* My first name is Miguel.

C Introduce the student to the rest of the class.

EXAMPLE:

This is Miguel. His last name is Oliveira. He speaks Portuguese.

LESSON 2 Greetings

GOAL ▶ Greet your friends

Life skill

A Juan and Michel work together. Read their conversation. Practice the conversation with a partner.

Juan: Good morning.
Michel: Morning!
Juan: How are you today?
Michel: Great! How about you?
Juan: Just fine.

B Use the expressions below to practice your own greetings. Greet three different classmates.

Greetings	Responses
Hi!	Hello!
Good morning!	Good morning to you, too!
How are you today?	Fine. / Great!
How's it going?	Pretty good.
How are you doing?	Not bad./O.K.
What's up?	Nothing.
What's new?	Not much.

C How would you express these words non-verbally (without words) in the United States? In your first country?

| Hello! | Goodbye! | Yes. | No. | I don't know. | Come here! |

3 Small talk

GOAL ▶ **Use small talk**

A Lara and Akiko are standing in line in the school cafeteria. How does Lara start the conversation?

Lara: Wow, the cafeteria is hot.
Akiko: It was very hot last summer, too.
Lara: Did you study here last summer?
Akiko: Yes. This is my second year.
Lara: What are you studying?
Akiko: I'm getting my AA in Business
Administration.

B Small talk is a way to start a conversation with people we don't know very well. Start some small talk with a partner. Choose a sentence below to begin the conversation. See how long you can keep the conversation going. Your teacher will tell you when to switch partners.

EXAMPLES:
- Did you watch the news last night?
- This weather is terrible!
- How was your weekend?
- It's busy here today.

C Some common topics for small talk are the weather, current events, and sports. Can you think of some other topics? Write them below.

_____

_____

D With a partner, create your own small talk conversation and present it to the class.

GOAL ▶ **Format a paragraph**

A Study the paragraph below. Notice the title, the margins, and the indented first line.

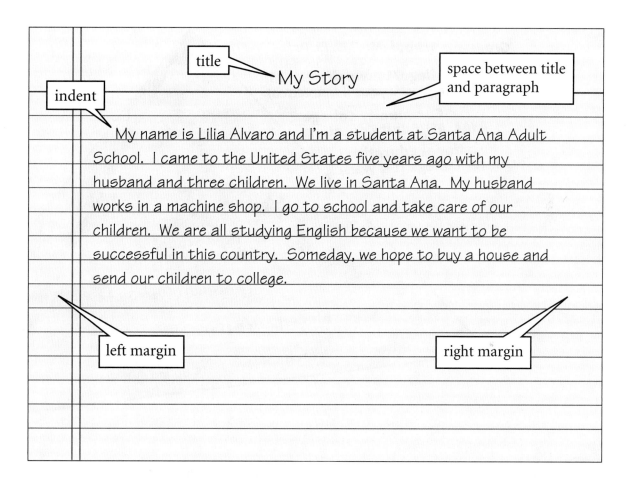

title — My Story

space between title and paragraph

indent

My name is Lilia Alvaro and I'm a student at Santa Ana Adult School. I came to the United States five years ago with my husband and three children. We live in Santa Ana. My husband works in a machine shop. I go to school and take care of our children. We are all studying English because we want to be successful in this country. Someday, we hope to buy a house and send our children to college.

left margin

right margin

B On a separate sheet of paper, write a paragraph about yourself using correct paragraph formatting. Use the paragraph above as a model.

C Show your paragraph to your partner. Ask questions about anything you want to know more about.

GOAL ▶ Discuss educational goals | *Vocabulary*

A This pyramid represents the educational system in the United States. Ask your teacher to explain the pyramid in detail.

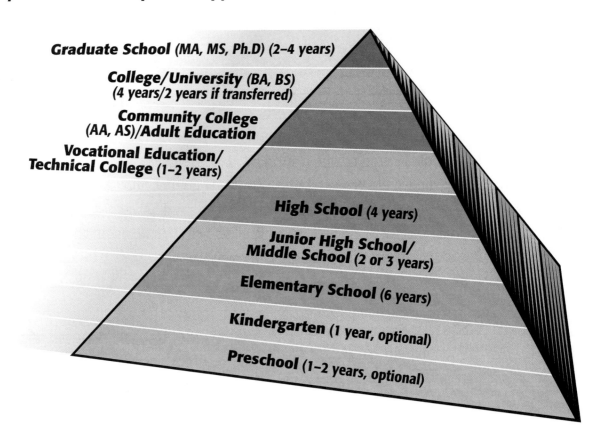

Graduate School (MA, MS, Ph.D) (2–4 years)

College/University (BA, BS) (4 years/2 years if transferred)

Community College (AA, AS)/**Adult Education**

Vocational Education/ Technical College (1–2 years)

High School (4 years)

Junior High School/ Middle School (2 or 3 years)

Elementary School (6 years)

Kindergarten (1 year, optional)

Preschool (1–2 years, optional)

B Where are you on the educational pyramid? Where do you want to be? How do you plan to get there?

C Discuss the educational pyramid with your teacher. How is the U. S. educational system different from the educational system in your first country?

D Draw a pyramid that shows your country's educational system on a separate sheet of paper. Then compare pyramids with a classmate.

UNIT 1

Balancing Your Life

GOALS

- Discuss schedules and routines
- Use future time clauses with *when*
- Write a paragraph
- Improve your study habits
- Use clauses with *because*
- Discuss values
- Use an outline

 **LESSON 1** Everyday life

GOAL ▶ Discuss schedules and routines   *Life skill*

A Look at Luisa's schedule. What are her routines?

	Monday	Tuesday	Wednesday	Thursday	Friday	Saturday	Sunday
Morning 6-8 A.M.	Go running	Go to grocery store	Go running	Clean house	Have breakfast with co-workers	Go running	
8-12 A.M./ P.M.	Day off	Work 10:00	Work 10:00	Work 10:00	Work 10:00	Work 10:00	Day off
Afternoon 12- 1 P.M.	Go shopping with Mary	Go to bank on lunch break				Go to library on lunch break	Have lunch with family
1-5 P.M.		Finish work 5:00	Finish work 5:00		Finish work 5:00	Finish work 5:00	
Evening 5-9 P.M.		ESL class 7-8	Computer class 6:30-7:30	Finish work 6:00	ESL class 7-8	Rent a video	

B Talk about Luisa's schedule with a partner. Ask questions using *What time . . . ? When . . . ?* and *What . . . ?*

EXAMPLE:
Student A: What time does Luisa start work?
Student B: She starts work at 10:00 A.M.

C Ask questions about Luisa's schedule using *How often . . . ?* Answer the questions using the frequency expressions in the box.

once a week	twice a week	three times a week	every morning
every weekday	every other day	every Saturday	on Fridays

EXAMPLE:
Student A: How often does Luisa rent a video?
Student B: Luisa rents a video every Saturday night.

D Where do you put these adverbs of frequency in a sentence? Study the rules and examples below.

0%	50%	100%

never	rarely	sometimes	usually	always

Frequency Adverbs	
Example	**Placement rule**
Luisa *always / usually / often* <u>goes</u> running. She *sometimes/ seldom / never* <u>makes</u> dinner.	Before the main verb
She <u>is</u> *usually* busy on the weekends.	After the main verb *be*
Usually / Sometimes Luisa studies in the library. Luisa studies in the library *sometimes / usually*.	*Sometimes / usually* can come at the beginning or at the end of a sentence.
Yes, I *always* <u>do</u>. / No, he *usually* <u>isn't</u>.	Between subject and verb in short answers
Correct: He *never* goes to the movies. Incorrect: ~~He doesn't never go to the movies.~~	*Rarely* and *never* are negative words. It is incorrect to use *not* with *rarely* or *never* in the same sentence.

E Make sentences about Luisa, using frequency adverbs. Follow the examples in the chart above.

F Make a schedule of everything you do in one week. Then talk about your schedule with your partner.

EXAMPLE: I never cook on my day off because I'm a cook in a restaurant!

LESSON 2 The future

GOAL ▶ **Use future time clauses with** *when*

Grammar

Zhou is worried about the future.
What is he thinking about?

A Read about Zhou.

Zhou's life is going to change very soon. His wife, Huixen, is going to have twins in July. His parents are going to come from China to live in the United States. He's happy, but his apartment will be too small for everyone. He needs a better job, but his boss won't promote him because he doesn't have a college degree.

Zhou has three goals. When his parents come to the United States, he will buy a two-family house. His father will work and help pay for the house. His mother will help take care of the children. Then he plans to go to night school and get a Bachelor's Degree. When he graduates, he will apply for a new position at work. He wants to work hard to achieve his goals.

B Read the story again and underline all the future forms.

will not
= won't

C After *when,* we usually use the present tense to talk about the future. Study this example.

When Zhou *graduates,* he *will* apply for a new position at work.
This sentence means:
First, he will graduate. *Then,* he will apply for a new position at work.

D **Look at the example and complete the sentences below with your own ideas.**

EXAMPLE:

When his parents *come* to the United States, Zhou's apartment *will* be too small.

1. When _____, they will buy a two-family house.

2. When Zhou's mother comes to stay, _____.

3. When _____, his boss will promote him.

4. When Zhou gets a better job, _____.

E **Look at Zhou's goals. He has personal goals (buy a new home), educational goals (graduate from college), and occupational goals (get a new position at work).**

F **What are your goals? Write them in the chart below.**

Personal	Educational	Occupational
Ex. get married	Ex. take an English course	Ex. get a raise at work
1. _____	1. _____	1. _____
2. _____	2. _____	2. _____
3. _____	3. _____	3. _____

G **With a group, discuss your future goals. Write sentences about your goals using *when*.**

EXAMPLE:

When I graduate, I will get a new job.

H **Active Task:** Type your goals on a sheet of paper and hang them up in a special place where you can read them each day.

 **Goals, obstacles, and solutions**

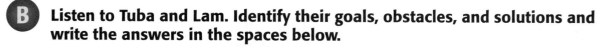 GOAL ▶ Write a paragraph | **Academic skill**

A **Read the paragraph and study the meaning of the words in italics.**

On the previous page, you wrote your *goals*. Goals are things we want to *achieve*. Sometimes we can have *problems* when we want to achieve our goals. These problems are called *obstacles*. When we find how to *solve* these problems, we have *solutions*.

 B **Listen to Tuba and Lam. Identify their goals, obstacles, and solutions and write the answers in the spaces below.**

Goal: Tuba wants to **_get a job to help her husband_**.

Obstacle: Her obstacle is _____.

Solutions:

1. Maybe she can _____.

2. Maybe her mother can _____.

Tuba

Goal: Lam wants to _____.

Obstacle: His obstacle is _____.

Solutions:

1. Maybe his grandchildren can _____.

2. Maybe his grandchildren can _____.

Lam

C **Choose one of the goals you wrote on page 4. Think of an *obstacle* and possible *solutions* and write them below.**

Goal: _____

Obstacle: _____

Solutions:

1. _____

2. _____

D **Share your sentences with a partner. Can your partner suggest other possible solutions?**

E **What is a paragraph? Discuss the following terms with your teacher.**

- A *paragraph* is a group of sentences about the *same topic*.

- A *topic sentence* is usually the first sentence and it introduces your *topic* or *main idea*.

- *Support sentences* are the sentences that follow your topic sentence. They give *details* about your topic.

- A *conclusion sentence* is the final sentence of your paragraph. It gives a *summary* of everything you wrote before.

F **On the previous page, you heard Tuba talk about her goal. Now read about her goal. Study the paragraph with your teacher.**

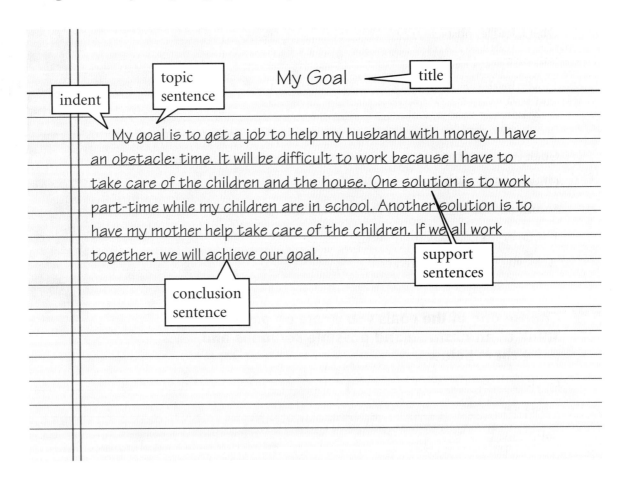

G **On a separate sheet of paper, write a paragraph about your goals, using correct paragraph formatting. Make sure your first sentence is a topic sentence. Follow your topic sentence with support sentences. Write a conclusion sentence at the end.**

LESSON 4 Study habits

GOAL ▶ **Improve your study habits**

A **Write answers to the following questions.**

1. Where do you like to study? _____

2. When do you usually study? _____

3. How long do you study? _____

4. Do you listen to music when you study? Why? Why not? _____

_____

B **Look at the first picture. What is Luisa doing? Do you think she is learning anything? Why or why not? Look at the second picture. What is Michel doing? Is he learning anything? Discuss your ideas with a partner.**

C Luisa needs to *improve* her study habits. Read the paragraphs below about study habits and then answer the questions that follow.

Good study habits can be very *beneficial* to you and your education. On the other hand, bad study habits can be *harmful* to your educational goals. First, let's talk about bad study habits.

Many people have very busy schedules, and it is difficult for them to find time to study. One bad study habit is not studying before class. Another bad study habit is studying with *distractions* around, such as television, people talking, or loud music. A third bad habit is copying a friend's homework. These are just a few bad study habits, but you can easily change them into good study habits.

There are many ways that you can improve your study habits. First, set a time every day to study and try to study at the same time every day. Do not make appointments at this time. This is your special study time. Second, find a good place to study, a place that is quiet and comfortable so that you can *concentrate*. Finally, do your homework on your own. Afterwards you can find a friend to help you *go over* your work and check your answers.

1. According to the reading, what are bad study habits? Write them below and add one more idea.

EXAMPLE:
Not studying before class

_____

_____

_____

2. According to the reading, what are good study habits? Write them below and add one more idea.

EXAMPLE:
Studying at the same time every day

_____

_____

_____

D Read the paragraphs in exercise C again. Try to work out the meaning of the words in italics by using the context (the words around the new word).

E Think about your study habits. Fill in the chart below and compare answers with a partner.

Good study habits	Bad study habits
1. I study every day.	1. I watch the news and do my homework at the same time.
2.	2.
3.	3.
4.	4.

F Match each vocabulary word on the left with its correct definition on the right.

_d_ 1. distractions   a. bad for you

____ 2. beneficial   b. get better

____ 3. harmful   c. review or check again

____ 4. improve   d. things that disturb your study

____ 5. concentrate   e. think hard about something

____ 6. go over   f. good for you

G Fill in the blanks in the sentences below with words from exercise F.

1. My English will _____ if I practice every day.

2. Please be quiet. I can't _____ on my homework.

3. Studying with a friend can be _____ because you can help each other.

4. When you finish taking a test, _____ your answers again.

5. It's hard to study when there are _____. Turn off the TV!

6. Bad study habits can be _____ to your educational goals.

H Choose three words from exercise F and write sentences about your study habits. Share your answers with a partner.

 I **Active Task:** Look up "good study habits" on the Internet or at the library. Find one useful idea and tell the class.

LESSON 5 Who is important to you?

GOAL ▶ Use clauses with *because* | **Grammar**

A Listen and identify the people in Luisa's wedding pictures.

sister-in-law / brother-in-law	co-worker	cousin
mother-in-law / father-in-law (in-laws)	godmother / godfather	partner
husband / wife (spouse)	aunt / uncle	friend

B Write the correct word next to each letter below. Use the words from the box to describe the relationship of the people in the pictures to Luisa.

a. _____   d. _____

b. _____   e. _____

c. _____   f. _____

C Who are the most important people in your life? List them and the reasons why they are important to you in the chart below.

Name	Relationship	Reason
Ex. Judy	mother	She taught me to be a good person.
1.		
2.		
3.		

D We use *because* to talk about reasons. Study the chart below.

Clauses with *because*	
Examples	**Rules**
My mother is very important to me <u>*because* she taught me to be a good person</u>. <u>*Because* my mother taught me to be a good person</u>, she is very important to me.	*Because* comes at the beginning of a clause. The *because* clause can come at the beginning or at the end of a sentence. When it comes at the beginning, use a comma. Use a pronoun (e.g., *he, she, they*) to avoid repeating the subject noun.

E Match the statements on the left with the reasons on the right. Then practice saying each sentence with a partner, reversing the clauses.

_*f*_ 1. I fell in love with my husband

____ 2. We asked Jenna to be Bob's godmother

____ 3. My sister is a single mother now

____ 4. I enjoy spending time with my friend

____ 5. My mother-in-law and I have a nice relationship

____ 6. You should ask your grandparents for advice

____ 7. Marco is in charge of the family business

____ 8. Pablo and his best friend are having a fight

a. because they have a lot of experience.

b. because she has good values.

c. because his parents are retired.

d. because she always makes me laugh.

e. because we respect each other.

f. because he is intelligent and kind.

g. because they both like the same girl.

h. because she got divorced.

F On a separate sheet of paper, write sentences about the most important people in your life, using *because*.

EXAMPLE:

<u>*My brother Daniel is important to me because he gives me good advice.*</u>

G **Read about the most important person in Luisa's life.**

The Most Important Person in My Life

The most important person in my life is my mother. She is very important to me because she raised me for 21 years. First of all, because she worked hard and was dedicated to her family, I always had a roof over my head and food on the table. Second, she taught me how to be a good person. She showed me by example how to treat others with kindness and myself with respect. Finally, whenever I had a problem, she was always there for me, listening to me and giving me good advice. No matter how far apart we are, my mother is always with me.

H **Write your own paragraph. Follow the steps below.**

1. Who is the most important person in your life? _____

2. *Brainstorming* is gathering your ideas before you write. Brainstorm reasons why this person is important to you. Write three reasons below.

   _____

   _____

   _____

3. A *topic sentence* tells your audience what you are writing about. Underline the topic sentence in the paragraph above. Write your own topic sentence.

   _____

4. A *conclusion* sentence is the final sentence in a paragraph. It repeats the idea from your introduction, using different words. Underline the conclusion sentence in the paragraph above. Write your own conclusion sentence below.

   _____

5. On a separate sheet of paper, write a paragraph about the most important person in your life. Start with your topic sentence, use the reasons from your brainstorming as support sentences, and finish with your conclusion sentence. Use the paragraph above as an example.

Things I value

GOAL ▶ **Discuss values**

What things are important to these people? What do they value?

A **Work in a group to make a list of things that people value.**

_____ _____

_____ _____

_____ _____

B **Choose three things from the list that are the most important to you. Write sentences explaining why these things are important. Use *because*.**

EXAMPLE:

I value education because it helps me to learn new skills.

Exercise is important to me because it improves my health.

_____

_____

_____

_____

C **Share your ideas with a partner by reading your sentences aloud.**

D **Complete each of the following statements, using the words from the box.**

friends	dog	education	bicycle
neighborhood	free time	children	teacher

1. The kids value their _____ because they feel safe there.

2. Long values his _____ because it guards the house.

3. Ellie values her _____ because they are always there when she needs them.

4. Jessika and Paul value their _____ because she gives them good advice.

5. Bud values his _____ because it helped him get a good job.

6. George values his _____ because they give him hope for the future.

7. Socorro values her _____ because it keeps her healthy.

8. Renata values her _____ because she likes to spend time with her family.

E **Ask some of your classmates what they value and why. Ask:** *What is your name? What do you value? Why?* **Write the information in the chart.**

Name	Value	Reason
Ex. Marco	books	They give him knowledge.
1.		
2.		
3.		
4.		

F **Write sentences about your classmates using the information in your chart.**

EXAMPLE: *Marco values his books because they give him knowledge.*

1. _____

2. _____

3. _____

4. _____

LESSON 7 Time management

GOAL ▶ **Use an outline**

Academic skill

A **Read about Lara's problem.**

The pie chart shows how Lara spends her time. She wants to be able to spend more time with her family. She rarely has free time to relax. Lara wants to find a way to balance her time, so she attends a lecture at school to learn time management skills.

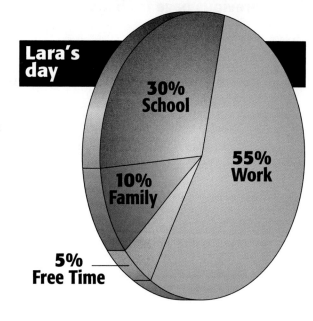

Lara's day

30% School

55% Work

10% Family

5% Free Time

B **Study the outline below. Listen to the lecture on time management and complete the sentences.**

I. Why is time management important?
   A. You stay organized.
   B. You accomplish everything that needs to get done.

   C. You _____.

II. How do you keep a schedule?
   A. Write down everything you need to do in a week.
   B. Put each task in a time slot.

   C. _____.
   D. Check off things that have been completed.

III. How can you add more time to your day?
   A. You can wake up earlier.

   B. You can ask _____.

   C. You can try doing _____ tasks at once.

IV. What are other important things to consider about time management?
   A. Remember the important people in your life.

   B. _____.
   C. You are the boss of your schedule.

V. What are the benefits of managing your time?
   A. You will have more free time.

   B. You will feel less _____.

   C. You will have time to _____.
   D. You will feel better about yourself.

C Fill in the pie chart on the right to show how you spend your time. Look at the pie chart on the previous page for help.

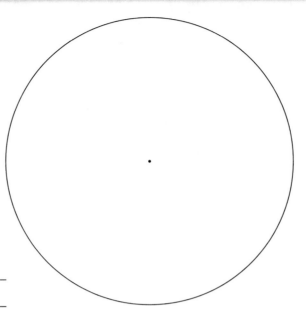

D Answer the following questions about your own time management strategies.

1. What problems do you have with time? (Example: I work 10 hours a day, so I don't have time to study.)

_____

_____

2. How could you add more time to your day? (Think about what you learned from the lecture.)

_____

_____

3. What are some time management skills you learned today that you would like to use in your life?

_____

_____

E What do the following expressions mean? Discuss them with your teacher.

to kill two birds with one stone	to waste time	to be on time
Time flies.	to find time	to run out of time
Time is money.	to make time	to spend time

F On a separate sheet of paper, write four sentences about your time management skills, using the expressions above.

G **Active Task:** Look up time management tips on the Internet or at the library. Find one useful tip and share it with the class.

Review

A Choose three words from this unit and write a definition for each word. Write the new words in your vocabulary notebook. Draw a picture next to each definition to help you remember the new words.

Goal - something I want to achieve

Obstacle - something that stops you from getting to your goal

Solution - a way to overcome the problem

B What do you do in your English class? Write sentences using each of the adverbs of frequency. Compare answers with a partner.

1. always _____

2. usually _____

3. often _____

4. sometimes _____

5. rarely _____

6. never _____

C What are your goals for the future? Look at the example and write three sentences about your future using *when*.

EXAMPLE: *When I finish this course, I will take the GED exam.*

1. _____.

2. _____.

3. _____.

D **Why is each of the following important? Draw a line from the word to the reason it is important. One reason is missing. Can you think of your own reason?**

A schedule   _____.

Goals   give me something to aim for.

Solutions   help me organize my time.

Good study habits   helps me remember what I need to do every day.

Relationships   help me to concentrate on my homework.

Time management skills   help me overcome obstacles.

E **Using the words and the reasons above, write five complete sentences using _because_.**

noun	pronoun
schedule	it
goals	they

EXAMPLE:

A schedule is important because _it helps me remember what I need to do every day._

1. _____

2. _____

3. _____

4. _____

5. _____

F **Think of one goal, obstacle, and solution that you have and complete the chart below. Then, on a separate sheet of paper, write a short paragraph about them.**

Goal	Obstacle	Solution

T E A M
P R O J E C T

Make a schedule

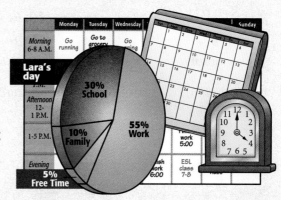

**With a team, you will design a blank weekly
schedule and discuss good time management
techniques. By yourself, you will think about
your goals and things that are important to
you and fill in the schedule based on your
personal goals.**

1. Form a team with four or five students. Choose
   positions for each member of your team.

Position	Job Description	Student Name
Student 1 Leader	See that everyone speaks English. See that everyone participates.	
Student 2 Secretary	Take notes on time management techniques.	
Student 3 Designer	Design schedule layout and add artwork.	
Students 4/5 Assistant(s)	Help secretary and designer with their work.	

2. With your team, design a blank weekly schedule and make a copy for each member in your group.

3. With your team, on a separate sheet of paper, make a list of time management techniques you'd like to use.

4. By yourself, on a separate piece of paper, make three lists:

   ● important people you need to spend time with each week (a visit, a letter, a phone call)

   ● things you would like to do during the week (exercise, read a book, take your children to the park)

   ● things you <u>have</u> to do (study English, go to the bank, pay bills)

5. Reread your list of time management techniques.

6. Fill in your personal schedule and include things from all three lists.

7. Share your completed schedule with your team. Is each student's schedule balanced? If not, give suggestions.

PRONUNCIATION

How many syllables are in each of these words? Which syllable is stressed in each word?

· ● ·

solution	conclusion	introduction	distraction	decision
relation	position	graduation	education	definition

LEARNER LOG

In this unit, you learned many things about balancing your life. How comfortable do you feel doing each of the skills listed below? Rate your comfort level on a scale of 1 to 4.

1 = Not so comfortable **2** = Need more practice **3** = Comfortable **4** = Very comfortable

If you circle 1 or 2, write down the page number where you can review this skill.

Life Skill	Comfort Level				Page(s)
I can discuss schedules and routines.	1	2	3	4	_____
I can discuss future goals, obstacles, and solutions.	1	2	3	4	_____
I can identify what is important to me.	1	2	3	4	_____
I can manage my time.	1	2	3	4	_____

Grammar					
I can use adverbs of frequency.	1	2	3	4	_____
I can use the future tense with *will* and *won't*.	1	2	3	4	_____
I can use future clauses with *when*.	1	2	3	4	_____
I can use clauses with *because*.	1	2	3	4	_____

Academic Skill					
I know how to improve study habits.	1	2	3	4	_____
I can write a paragraph.	1	2	3	4	_____
I can listen to a lecture and use an outline.	1	2	3	4	_____

Reflection

1. What was the most useful thing you learned in this unit? _____

_____

2. How will this help you in life? _____

_____

Consumer Smarts

GOALS

- Identify places to buy goods and services
- Fill out a credit card application
- Interpret advertisements
- Use comparatives and superlatives
- Express opinions about goods and services
- Interpret product labels
- Use sequencing transitions

LESSON 1 Shopping for goods and services

GOAL ▶ Identify places to buy goods and services   *Vocabulary*

A What kind of stores or businesses are these? What goods or services can you buy here?

B Look at the places below. Which of them sell goods? Which of them provide services? Make two lists.

laundromat	gas station	pharmacy	bank
post office	department store	hotel	appliance store
office supply store	car wash	tailor	ophthalmologist

C Where can you buy each of the following items? Write the name of the store in the chart below. Some items may have more than one answer.

Item	Place	Item	Place
1. medicine	a. pharmacy	6. a refrigerator	f.
2. a table	b.	7. bread	g.
3. a notebook	c.	8. motor oil	h.
4. a hammer	d.	9. a CD	i.
5. boots	e.	10. some stamps	j.

D We can use the expression *to get something done* when we talk about services we receive. Study the chart with your teacher.

To get something done				
Subject	*get*	Object	Past participle	Example sentence
I	get	my hair	cut	I get my hair cut every month.
she	got	her clothes	cleaned	She got her clothes cleaned yesterday.

E Where can you receive the following services? Write the name of the business on the line below. There may be more than one answer.

EXAMPLE: get your clothes cleaned **_dry cleaner_**

1. get your hair cut _____

2. get your checks cashed _____

3. get your eyes tested _____

4. get your car washed _____

5. get your car fixed _____

6. get your clothes washed _____

F Imagine you are new to the neighborhood. Ask your partner questions about businesses in the area.

EXAMPLE:
Student A: Where can I get my car washed?   *Student B:* At the car wash on Maple Street.

G **Active Task:** Go to a mall and look at a directory. What different stores and businesses does it have?

LESSON 2 Cash or charge?

GOAL ▶ **Fill out a credit card application** | *Life skill*

A **Ali uses four different ways to make purchases. What are they?**

B **Write the correct word next to its description.**

cash	personal check	credit card	debit card

1. This is a form you fill out asking your bank to pay money out of your account.

   _____

2. This allows you to borrow money to make purchases. _____

3. Coins and bills are this. _____

4. This allows a store to take money directly from your account to pay for purchases.

   _____

C **With a group, think of advantages and disadvantages for each purchasing method.**

EXAMPLE:
Student A: Cash is good because it is quick and easy.
Student B: Yes, but if you lose cash, you cannot replace it.

D **Talk to a partner about the payment method you prefer and why.**

E In order to get a credit card, you need to fill out an application with personal information. Below is a list of Ali's personal information. Draw a line to match each piece of information on the left with the description on the right.

5453 Leilani Lane	city, state, zip code
$40, 000	date of birth
Houston, TX 90742	address
E & E Electronics	annual household income
Ali Abdullah Mohammoud	home phone number
10 / 13 / 75	full name
XXX–XX–XXXX	employer
(713) 555–7928	social security number

F Use the information above to fill out the credit card application below for Ali.

🏛 **Fairfield Bank**
Credit Card Application

Full Name: ⎵⎵⎵⎵⎵⎵⎵⎵⎵⎵⎵⎵⎵⎵⎵⎵⎵⎵⎵⎵⎵⎵⎵⎵⎵⎵⎵⎵⎵⎵⎵⎵⎵⎵⎵⎵⎵

Address: ⎵⎵⎵⎵⎵⎵⎵⎵⎵⎵⎵⎵⎵⎵⎵⎵⎵⎵⎵⎵⎵⎵⎵⎵⎵⎵⎵⎵⎵⎵⎵⎵⎵⎵⎵⎵⎵

City: ⎵⎵⎵⎵⎵⎵⎵⎵⎵⎵⎵⎵⎵⎵⎵⎵ State: ⎵⎵ Zip Code: ⎵⎵⎵⎵⎵-⎵⎵⎵⎵

Number of Years at Residence: ⎵2⎵   Social Security Number: ⎵⎵⎵-⎵⎵-⎵⎵⎵⎵

Date of Birth (mm/dd/yy): ⎵⎵/⎵⎵/⎵⎵

Home Phone: (⎵⎵⎵)-⎵⎵⎵-⎵⎵⎵⎵   Work Phone: (⎵⎵⎵)-⎵⎵⎵-⎵⎵⎵⎵

Employer Name: ⎵⎵⎵⎵⎵⎵⎵⎵⎵⎵⎵⎵⎵⎵⎵⎵⎵⎵⎵⎵⎵⎵⎵⎵⎵⎵

Years at Employer: ⎵5⎵   Annual Household Income: $ ⎵⎵⎵⎵⎵⎵⎵

  G **Active Task:** Print out a credit card application from the Internet or get an application from your bank and fill it out. (Don't send it, unless you really want the card!)

LESSON 3 Advertisements

GOAL ▶ Interpret advertisements | ***Life skill***

A **Discuss the following questions with your class. What are advertisements? Where can you find them? What information can you find in advertisements?**

B **Read the advertisements from the newspaper.**

1.

2.

3.

4.

C **Read the ads again and find words with these meanings.**

discount ___*on sale*___

guarantee ______________

work ______________

to come to an end ______________

no charge ______________

approximate cost ______________

set up for use ______________

usual ______________

D **Read the ads again and fill in the circle next to the correct answer.**

1. What does the oil change NOT include?
   ○ oil   ○ oil filter   ○ windshield wiper fluid

2. When does the offer expire for the oil change?
   ○ May 8, 2003   ○ August 8, 2003   ○ August 5, 2003

3. When does the garage door sale end?
   ○ February 12, 2003   ○ December 2, 2003   ○ February 2, 2003

4. What does the garage door purchase NOT include?
   ○ new door installation   ○ removal of old door   ○ 3-year warranty

5. How do you get an in-home estimate for a new garage door?
   ○ call   ○ go to the company   ○ write a letter

6. What is for sale at the stereo factory outlet?
   ○ stereo speakers   ○ headphones   ○ stereo speakers and headphones

7. What is the discount at the outlet?
   ○ $9.95   ○ 30–70 percent   ○ $79.95

8. What is the regular price of the bikes?
   ○ $150.00   ○ $112.50   ○ $250.00

9. How much are the bikes discounted?
   ○ $25   ○ 25%   ○ $37.00

10. Which item(s) come with a warranty?
    ○ garage doors   ○ bicycles   ○ garage doors and bicycles

E **With a group of students, choose a product and create an advertisement for it. Remember to include the name of your company, the name of your product, a small picture, and details of prices and discounts.**

F **Active Task:** Find some newspaper advertisements and bring them to class. What special offers can you find?

LESSON 4 Making comparisons

GOAL ▶ **Use comparatives and superlatives** | *Grammar*

A Do you have a computer? Do you know someone who has a computer? Think of the different parts of a computer. What do you use them for? Use the words from the box to label the picture.

monitor	mouse	screen	mouse pad
CD-ROM drive	keyboard	CPU	floppy drive

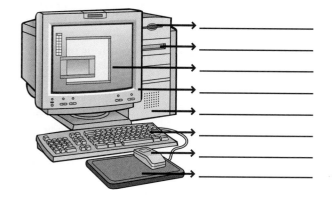

CPU = Central Processing Unit

GHz = Gigahertz

MHz = Megahertz

1,000 MHz = 1 GHz

MB = Megabytes

15″ = 15 inches

B **What should you look for when you buy a computer?**

Speed: Is the computer *fast* or *slow?*
Monitor: Is the monitor *large* or *small?*
Memory: How *big* is the memory?
Price: Is the computer *expensive* or *cheap?*

C Study the information about five different computers. Use the adjectives above to talk about them.

EXAMPLE: The JCN computer has a large monitor.

	JCN	Doshina	Vintel	Shepland	Kontaq
Price	$1599	$2599	$1649	$1499	$999
Speed	1 Ghz	1.4 GHz	1.2 GHz	1 GHz	667 MHz
Monitor size	17″	18″	20″	14″	16″
Memory	192 MB	256 MB	192 MB	128 MB	64 MB

D **Study the chart with your teacher.**

Comparatives				
	Adjective	**Comparative**	**Rule**	**Example sentence**
Short adjectives (one or two syllables)	cheap	cheaper	Add *-er* to the end of the adjective.	Your computer was *cheaper* than my computer.
Long adjectives (three or more syllables)	expensive	more expensive	Add *more* before the adjective.	The new computer was *more expensive* than my old one.
Irregular adjectives	good bad	better worse	These adjectives are irregular.	The computer at school is *better* than this one.

Remember to use *than* after a comparative adjective followed by a noun or pronoun.

E **Use the rules above to make comparative adjectives.**

> **Spelling rule:**
> hot–hotter
> easy–easier
> large–larger

EXAMPLE: slow _____*slower*_____

small _____   fast _____

wide _____   beautiful _____

big _____   interesting _____

bad _____   friendly _____

F **Make sentences about the computers on page 27.**

EXAMPLE: The Kontaq / slow / the Vintel
The Kontaq is slower than the Vintel.

1. The JCN monitor / large / the Shepland monitor

_____

2. The Doshina / fast / the Vintel

_____

3. The Vintel's memory / big / the Kontaq

_____

4. The Doshina / expensive / the Shepland

_____

G **Talk to your partner. Which computer from page 27 would you buy? Give three reasons, using comparatives.**

H Study the chart with your teacher.

Superlatives				
	Adjective	**Superlative**	**Rule**	**Example sentence**
Short adjectives (one or two syllables)	cheap	the cheapest	Add -*est* to the end of the adjective.	Your computer is *the cheapest.*
Long adjectives (three or more syllables)	expensive	the most expensive	Add *most* before the adjective.	He bought *the most expensive* computer in the store.
Irregular adjectives	good bad	the best the worst	These adjectives are irregular.	The computers at school are *the best.*

Always use *the* before a superlative followed by a noun or pronoun.

I Use the rules above to make superlative adjectives.

EXAMPLE: slow ____*the slowest*____

> **Spelling rule:**
> hot–the hottest
> easy–the easiest
> large–the largest

small _____   fast _____

wide _____   beautiful _____

big _____   interesting _____

good _____   friendly _____

J Look at the computers on page 27 and make sentences.

EXAMPLE:
fast / The Doshina computer is the fastest.
wide / The Vintel computer has the widest screen.

1. expensive _____

2. cheap _____

3. slow _____

4. big memory _____

5. small memory _____

  K **Active Task:** Look at some advertisements for computers in magazines or on the Internet and make comparative and superlative statements about what the ads say.

LESSON 5 A good buy?

| GOAL ▶ Express opinions about goods and services | *Life skill* |

A Listen to the following statements made by consumers. In the table below, write down what these consumers bought and their opinions about the product, service, or experience.

Consumer	Product/Service	Opinion
Ex. Janie	shoes	cute but uncomfortable
1. Thomas		
2. Rosa		
3. Nicolai		
4. Yen		

B Look at the list of adjectives below. Discuss the meanings with your teacher.

☺ Good		☺ Fair		☹ Bad	
wonderful	great	OK	average	awful	terrible
amazing	delicious	so-so	not bad	horrible	dreadful
incredible	awesome	mediocre			

C Read the conversation below. What adjectives could fit in the blanks?

Student A: Did you have a good time last night?

Student B: We had a(n) _____ time at the movies.

Student A: Tell me about it.

Student B: The movie was _____ and the popcorn

was _____.

D With a partner, practice the conversation. Choose adjectives from the list to complete the sentences.

E What are some products that you bought recently? Write them in the chart below. What adjectives can you use to describe these products? Write two positive and two negative adjectives after each product.

Product	Positive	Negative
couch	comfortable, soft	uncomfortable, expensive

F Use the information from the table to practice the conversations below with a partner.

EXAMPLE:
Student A: I really like your new **_couch_**!
Student B: Thanks! Isn't it **_comfortable_**?

Student A: I really like your new _____!

Student B: Thanks! Isn't it / Aren't they _____?

Student A: I don't like that/those _____ at all.

Student B: I know! Isn't it/aren't they _____?

G Imagine you are in the situations below. What would you say? Practice the conversations with a partner.

EXAMPLE:
Student A: I am not going back to that restaurant.
Student B: Why not?
Student A: The food was really awful.

1. You just finished eating at a restaurant.
2. You and your friend are in a clothing store looking at jackets.
3. You and your cousin just took your car in for service.

6 Reading product labels

GOAL ▶ Interpret product labels   *Life skill*

A What information can you find on a product label? Make a list with your class.

B Study the verbs in the box below.

| measure | wipe | wet | rub | squeeze | rinse | spray | shake |

C Match each of the products with its label. Write the correct letter next to each label.

a.

b.

c.

d.

Directions: Measure with cup and add to water with detergent. Wash and rinse clothes as usual. Use for white clothes only.

1. ___*d*___

Directions: Shake bottle before using. Add 10–12 drops to 1 pint of water when you water your indoor plants. Just squeeze the bottle to release the drops. Replace cap tightly when finished.

3. _____

Directions: Wet surface. Sprinkle on cloth. Rub area in a circle with cloth. Wait for 10–15 minutes. Wipe with a clean wet cloth. Do not use on windows or mirrors. Repeat if necessary.

2. _____

Directions: Spray 5–7 inches from surface. Wipe clean with a dry towel.

4. _____

D **Which products on page 32 might have a warning? Read the warnings below and match them with the correct picture.**

1. __b__ Do not use near heat or flame.

2. _____ Avoid contact with eyes.

3. _____ Always wear gloves.

4. _____ Keep out of reach of children.

5. _____ Poison. Do not swallow.

6. _____ Do not inhale.

a.

b.

c.

d.

e.

f.

E **Study the chart with your teacher. We use *imperatives* to give commands or warnings.**

Infinitive	Imperative	Example sentence
to wear	wear	Always *wear* gloves.
to use	do not use	*Do not use* near fire.

F **Reread the labels on page 32. Underline the imperatives.**

G Using imperatives, write instructions on how to use oven cleaner. Then write a warning. Write your sentences next to each picture.

1. ___*Wear rubber gloves.*___

2. _____

3. _____

4. _____

Warning: _____

H Now give your friend instructions for the following products. Give a warning if necessary!

1. shampoo   2. wood polish   3. carpet cleaner   4. dental floss

 I **Active Task:** Find some products in your home or look them up on the Internet and read the product labels. What kind of warnings do they have? Tell the class.

Steps to a smart purchase

GOAL ▶ Use sequencing transitions

Academic skill

What is Ali doing?
What things should you compare
before buying a product?

 A **Read about smart purchases below.**

Making a Smart Purchase

You make a smart purchase when you think and plan before you buy something. First of all, you make a decision to buy something. This is the easy part. The second step is comparison shopping. You comparison shop by reading advertisements, going to different stores, and talking to friends and family. Third, you choose which product you are going to buy. Which is the best deal? Do you have enough money to buy this product? If you don't, the next step is to start saving. This may take a while, depending on how much you need to save. Once you have enough money, you are ready to make your purchase. If you follow these steps to make a purchase, you will be a smart consumer. And smart consumers make smart purchases!

B **Put the following steps in order from 1 to 5 according to the paragraph above.**

_____ Make the purchase.   __*1*__ Decide to buy something.   _____ Save money.

_____ Read advertisements.   _____ Choose the best deal.

C **Rewrite the above steps after each of the phrases below.**

First, **_decide to buy something_**.

Second, _____

Next, _____

Then, _____

Finally, _____

D *Sequencing transitions* are used to describe stages of a process. Study the examples in the box below.

First,	First of all,	Second,	Second of all,	Third,
Fourth,	Next,	Then,	Lastly,	Finally,

E Read the following paragraph and write an appropriate sequencing transition in each blank. There may be more than one correct answer.

How to Plant a Seed

_____, buy some seeds and a pot to put them in. _____, put dirt in the pot. _____, dig a small hole in the dirt.

_____, carefully put the seeds in the hole. Gently cover the seeds. _____, water the dirt. _____, put the pot in a sunny place and watch your flowers grow.

F Underline the imperatives in the paragraph above.

G Choose one of these processes and write a paragraph describing how to do it.

1. check your e-mail
2. wash a car
3. use an ATM machine
4. get a driver's license

H **Active Task:** Teach one of the above processes to a family member or to your classmates and teacher.

Review

A **Make flash cards to improve your vocabulary.**

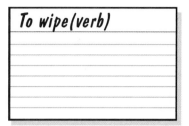

To wipe (verb)

1. Choose seven words from this unit.

2. Write each word on a card or piece of paper.

3. On the back, write a definition or a sentence with the word missing and a picture.

4. Study the words while you are traveling to school or work, or read them during breakfast. (Remember your time management skills!)

5. Do this for each unit, and add other new words that you learn in or out of class. If you study a little each day, you will improve your vocabulary very quickly.

_____ the window.

B **Imagine you are preparing for a big event: a job interview, a party at your house, or a wedding in another state. Make a list of the things you need to do to get ready for the event. Then write where you will go to complete the errand. Compare lists with a partner.**

Event	Things to do	Places to get these goods or services

C **When do you use the following? Write the correct letter next to each number.**

____ 1. imperatives

____ 2. comparative adjectives

____ 3. superlative adjectives

____ 4. sequencing transitions

a. to compare one thing to a group of things

b. to connect steps in a process

c. to give commands or instructions

d. to compare one thing to another

Review

D Choose one of the following processes and write a paragraph describing how to do it using sequencing transitions. Ask a partner to act out the steps as you read them aloud. Were the instructions clear and easy to follow?

1. make coffee   2. wash the dishes   3. plant a tree in the backyard

E Complete the following statements with a comparative or a superlative adjective.

EXAMPLE:

My new watch is ***cheaper than*** my old watch. (cheap)

1. Emir is _____ runner on the team. (fast)

2. My sister, Regiane, is _____ my brother. (tall)

3. This box is much _____ that one. What's in it? (heavy)

4. _____ sunsets in the world are in Hawaii. (beautiful)

5. Do you think that the book is _____ the movie? (interesting)

6. School is hard now. I am _____ I was last semester. (busy)

7. My neighbor's house is _____ our house. (big)

8. Do you think their team is _____ your team? (good)

F Imagine you are going to buy a new car–your dream car. Write sentences comparing your old car to your new car.

EXAMPLE:

My new car is faster than my old car.

_____

_____

_____

G What is the best restaurant in your neighborhood? Write sentences comparing this restaurant to all the other restaurants in the neighborhood.

EXAMPLE:

China Palace has the friendliest service in the neighborhood.

_____

_____

_____

TEAM
PROJECT

Market a product

With a team, you will create a product label and advertisement and present your product to the class.

1. Form a team with four or five students. Choose positions for each member of your team.

Position	Job Description	Student Name
Student 1 Leader	See that everyone speaks English. See that everyone participates.	
Student 2 Secretary	Write information for label and advertisement.	
Student 3 Designer	Design product and advertisement layout.	
Students 4/5 Assistant(s)	Help secretary and designer with their work.	

2. With your team, choose a product and think of a name for that product.

3. Create a label for your product, including instructions for use and appropriate warnings.

4. Create a print advertisement for your product. Include pictures.

5. Present your product and advertisement to the class.

PRONUNCIATION

Listen carefully to the intonation of these expressions. How does the speaker's voice go up or down to show that she is feeling positive or negative? Listen again and repeat. Draw arrows to show the intonation.

1. The food was wonderful!   3. The movie was awful.   5. The hotel was O.K.

2. The book was incredible!   4. The music was terrible.   6. The game was so-so.

LEARNER LOG

In this unit, you learned many things about consumer smarts. How comfortable do you feel doing each of the skills listed below? Rate your comfort level on a scale of 1 to 4.

1 = Not so comfortable **2** = Need more practice **3** = Comfortable **4** = Very comfortable

If you circle 1 or 2, write down the page number where you can review this skill.

Life Skill	Comfort Level				Page(s)
I can identify places to purchase goods and services.	1	2	3	4	_____
I can describe reasons for using different purchasing methods.	1	2	3	4	_____
I can interpret advertisements.	1	2	3	4	_____
I can express opinions about goods and services.	1	2	3	4	_____
I can understand product labels and directions.	1	2	3	4	_____
I can give instructions.	1	2	3	4	_____
I can understand sequence of instructions.	1	2	3	4	_____

Grammar

I can use comparative and superlative adjectives.	1	2	3	4	_____
I can use imperatives.	1	2	3	4	_____

Academic Skill

I can interpret and understand steps in a process.	1	2	3	4	_____
I can use sequencing transitions.	1	2	3	4	_____

Reflection

1. What was the most useful thing you learned in this unit? _____

_____

2. How will this help you in life? _____

_____

UNIT 3 Housing

GOALS

- Interpret classified ads
- Make decisions about housing
- Understand a rental agreement
- Arrange and cancel utilities by phone
- Use the past continuous
- Write a letter to your landlord
- Make a budget

LESSON 1 House hunting

GOAL ▶ Interpret classified ads   **Life skill**

A Think about the place where you live. How did you find it? What are some different ways to find housing?

B One way to find housing is through *classified ads* in the newspaper. Read the ads below. Which apartment do you like best?

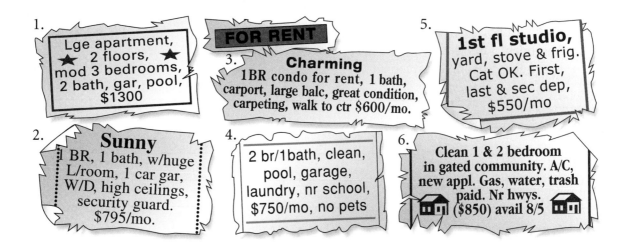

1. Lge apartment, ★ 2 floors, ★ mod 3 bedrooms, 2 bath, gar, pool, $1300

FOR RENT

3. **Charming** 1BR condo for rent, 1 bath, carport, large balc, great condition, carpeting, walk to ctr $600/mo.

5. **1st fl studio,** yard, stove & frig. Cat OK. First, last & sec dep, $550/mo

2. **Sunny** 1 BR, 1 bath, w/huge L/room, 1 car gar, W/D, high ceilings, security guard. $795/mo.

4. 2 br/1bath, clean, pool, garage, laundry, nr school, $750/mo, no pets

6. Clean 1 & 2 bedroom in gated community. A/C, new appl. Gas, water, trash paid. Nr hwys. ($850) avail 8/5

C Make a list of the abbreviations in the ads. What does each abbreviation stand for? Discuss their meanings with your teacher.

D **Discuss the following questions about housing with your partner.**

1. How many rooms are in a studio apartment?
2. What is the difference between an apartment and a condominium?
3. What other names for different types of housing do you know?

E **Here is another way to make comparisons. Study the charts below.**

Comparatives using nouns	
Our new apartment has *more bedrooms* than our old one.	Use *more* or *fewer* to compare count nouns.
Our old apartment had *fewer bedrooms* than our new one.	
Rachel's apartment gets *more light* than Pablo's apartment.	Use *more* or *less* to compare non-count nouns.
Pablo's apartment gets *less light* than Rachel's apartment.	

Superlatives using nouns	
Rachel's apartment has *the most bedrooms*.	Use *the most* or *the fewest* for count nouns.
Phuong's apartment has *the fewest bedrooms*.	
Rachel's apartment gets *the most light*.	Use *the most* or *the least* for non-count nouns.
Phuong's apartment gets *the least light*.	

F **Write six sentences comparing the apartments on the previous page. Compare: light, bathrooms, appliances, and services.**

EXAMPLES:
Apartment 1 has more rooms than apartment 2.
Apartment 1 has the most rooms.

1. _____
2. _____
3. _____
4. _____
5. _____
6. _____

 G **Active Task:** Read classified ads for housing in a newspaper or on the Internet. What abbreviations can you find? Tell the class.

GOAL ▶ **Make decisions about housing**

Life skill

A **Read about the Nguyen family.**

The Nguyen family lives in Cedarville, Texas. Vu Nguyen came from Vietnam twenty years ago and met his wife, Maryanne, in Texas. The Nguyens have four children—two sons and two daughters. They are currently living in a two-bedroom apartment, which is too small for all six of them. They would like to stay in Cedarville, but they need a bigger place. Vu recently got a raise at work, so the Nguyen family wants to move.

B **Listen to the Nguyen family talk about their housing preferences. Put a check in the box next to the things they would like to have in their new apartment.**

☐ 2 bedrooms	☐ tennis courts	☐ yard
☐ 3 bedrooms	☐ pool	☐ air conditioning
☐ 2 bathrooms	☐ security guard	☐ carpeting
☐ 3 bathrooms	☐ big windows	☐ balcony
☐ type of heating	☐ carport	☐ washer/dryer

C **Compare your answers with a partner.**

D Study the chart with your teacher.

Yes/No questions and answers with *do/does*				
Questions				**Answers**
do	**Subject**	**Base**	**Example question**	
do	I, you, we, they	have	Do they have a yard?	Yes, they do. / No, they don't.
does	he, she, it	want	Does she want air conditioning?	Yes, she does. / No, she doesn't.

E Practice asking questions with a partner, using the Nguyen family's preferences on the previous page.

EXAMPLE:
Student A: Do they want five bedrooms?
Student B: No, they don't.

F Imagine you are going to buy or rent a new home. What kind of home do you want? Check your preferences below. Add any items that are not on the list.

Yes No

☐ ☐ ___ bedrooms
☐ ☐ ___ bathrooms
☐ ☐ yard
☐ ☐ balcony
☐ ☐ pool
☐ ☐ washer/dryer

Yes No

☐ ☐ air conditioning
☐ ☐ heating
☐ ☐ garage
☐ ☐ carport
☐ ☐ refrigerator
☐ ☐ _____

G Practice asking questions to a partner about his or her housing preferences.

EXAMPLE:
Student A: Do you want a garage?
Student B: Yes, I do.

LESSON 3 Landlords and tenants

GOAL ▶ **Understand a rental agreement**

A Do you have a rental agreement for the place you are living in now? What information is on a rental agreement?

B Review the rental agreement below. Your teacher will help you with key vocabulary.

---

1. The parties to this agreement are:

Landlord(s): _____

Address: _____

Phone: _____

Tenant(s): _____

Phone: Home: _____ Work: _____

2. The property leased by Landlord to Tenant is located at:

_____

and includes the following furniture and/or appliances:

_____

_____

3. This agreement is: ☐ a lease for a term of _____ months beginning on _____ and ending on _____ or ☐ from month to month.

4. The monthly rental fee shall be $_____ per month, due and payable on the _____ day of each month.

5. Utilities shall be paid as follows:

	Landlord	Tenant
Electricity	_____	**X**
Gas	_____	**X**
Water	**X**	_____

6. Landlord acknowledges receipt of a ☐ deposit ☐ nonrefundable fee in the amount of $ _____ .

Upon termination of the tenancy, any refund to the deposit is conditioned upon:

_____

_____

The Undersigned acknowledge that they have read the rental agreement and will comply with its terms.

Landlord(s): _____ Date: _____

Tenant(s): _____ Date: _____

C **Read each of the following statements and decide which section of the rental agreement on page 45 it applies to. Write the correct number after the statement. Then fill in the rental agreement with the correct information.**

EXAMPLE:
The landlord will pay for water and the Nguyen family will pay for gas and electricity. __5__

1. The Nguyens will pay a security deposit of $500. They will get the money back if the apartment is

   in good condition when they leave. _____

2. The landlord is John Nassab and his address is 9468 Millbank Road, Orange, TX 77042. His

   phone number is (713) 555-9782. _____

3. The Nguyens will rent month to month. _____

4. The tenants are Maryanne, Vu, Bao, Truyen, Nga, and Truc Nguyen. Their home phone number is

   (713) 555-1372 and Vu's work number is (713) 555-8316. _____

5. The Nguyens will pay $1350 on the first day of each month. _____

6. Their apartment includes a washer and dryer and a refrigerator. _____

7. The Nguyens' new apartment is located at 5829 Bay Road, Cedarville, TX 77041. _____

D **Change the following statements into *yes/no* questions using *do* or *does*.**

EXAMPLE:
The Nguyens rent month to month.
Do the Nguyens rent month to month?

1. The apartment includes a refrigerator.

   _____

2. The landlord pays for water.

   _____

3. Maryanne and Vu pay for water.

   _____

4. Maryanne and Vu need to pay a deposit of $500.

   _____

E **Ask a partner the questions in exercise D. Your partner will give you short answers.**

EXAMPLE:
Student A: Do the Nguyens rent month to month?   *Student B:* Yes, they do.

F **Active Task:** Review the rental agreement for your home.

GOAL ▶ **Arrange and cancel utilities by phone** | **Life skill**

 A **Discuss the following questions with your teacher.**

1. What are utilities?
2. What utilities do you pay for?
3. Does your landlord pay for any utilities?
4. What information can you find on your utility bills?

Southern Texas Gas P.O. Box D Cedarville, TX 77014	Service Address Vu Nguyen 3324 Maple Road Cedarville, TX 77014	Account Number 891 007 1087 5	Billing Period 5/26/02–6/28/02
		Readings	Next meter reading
		prev 4226 pres 4251	Jul 28, 2002

SUMMARY OF CHARGES

Customer Charge	33 days	×	0.16438 =	5.42
Baseline	15 Therms	×	0.65133 =	9.77
Over Baseline	10 Therms	×	0.82900 =	8.29
Gas Charges				23.48
State Regulatory Fee	25 Therms	×	0.00076 =	.02
Taxes and Fees on Gas Charges				.02
Total Gas Charges Including Taxes and Fees				$23.52

Thank you for your payment Jun 06, 2002 $27.65

Total Amount Due   **$23.52**
Current Amount Past Due if not paid by Jul 21, 2002

 B **Read the gas bill and answer the questions below.**

1. What is the Nguyen family's account number? _____

2. How much is their gas bill this month? _____

3. Check the total amount of their bill. Is it correct? _____

4. How much did they pay last month? _____

5. Which bill was more expensive—this month's or last month's? _____

6. When is the payment due? _____

Have you ever phoned a utility company?
What happened?

  C **Vu and his family are getting ready to move. Vu calls the electric company to speak to a customer service representative. Read the conversation as you listen to the recording.**

Recording: Thank you for calling Texas Electric. Your call is very important to us. Please choose from the following options. For new service or to cancel your existing service, press *1*. To report a problem with your service, press *2*. If you have questions about your bill, press *3*. For all other questions, press *4*. Thank you. Just one moment.

Representative: Hello, my name is Kristen. How may I help you?
Vu: Um, yes. My family is moving next week and we need to cancel our current service and get service in our new home.

Representative: What is your current address?
Vu: 3324 Maple Road.

Representative: Are you Vu Nguyen?
Vu: Yes.

Representative: When would you like the service turned off?
Vu: Next Wednesday, please.

Representative: And what is your new address?
Vu: 5829 Bay Road.

Representative: And when would you like the service turned on?
Vu: This Monday, please.

Representative: O.K. Your current service will be turned off sometime between 8 A.M. and 12 noon on Wednesday the 11th and your new service will be on before 9 A.M. on Monday morning the 9th. Is there anything else I can do for you?
Vu: No, that's it.

Representative: Thank you for calling Texas Electric. Have a nice day.
Vu: You, too.

D **Listen to the recording again and answer the questions. Try not to look at the script this time.**

1. The first voice is recorded and gives you four choices. What are they?

   a. *get new service or cancel existing service* _____

   b. _____

   c. _____

   d. _____

2. What information does Vu give to the electric company?

   a. *his current address* _____

   b. _____

   c. _____

   d. _____

E **Imagine you are moving. Write down your current address and a possible new address. What date will you leave your old home and what date will you move to your new home? With a partner, practice Vu's conversation with the electric company using your own information.**

Current address	New address	Date leaving current address	Date moving into new home

F **With a partner, discuss ways to reduce the cost of your electric bill. What can you do to save energy?**

G **Active Task:** Look on the Internet for energy saving tips. Call the gas or electric company and ask them to send some information.

GOAL ▶ **Use the past continuous** | **Grammar**

A **Look at the pictures below. Do you ever have these problems in your home? Do you fix the problems yourself or do you call someone?**

a. The air conditioner isn't working.

c. There are roaches and mice in the kitchen.

b. The electricity went out.

d. The faucet is leaking.

B **Who can you call to fix each problem? Match the person with the problem.**

_b_ 1. electrician ____ 2. exterminator ____ 3. repairperson ____ 4. plumber

C **Practice the conversation with a partner. You can add your own situations as well.**

Tenant: Hello, Mr./Mrs. Jones. This is <u>John</u> in apartment 3B.
Landlord: Hi, <u>John</u>. What can I do for you?
Tenant: The air conditioning in our apartment isn't working. *(State the problem.)*
Landlord: O.K. I'll send a repairperson over to fix it tomorrow. *(State the solution.)*
Tenant: Thanks.

Indira had a bad night in her apartment. Read about what happened.

    I had a terrible night. While I was making dinner, I saw a mouse. Then the electricity went out while I was studying. It was dark, so I went to bed. But I couldn't sleep. The faucet was dripping all night. And the neighbors were shouting, and their dog was barking. Perhaps I should move!

E **Study the chart. Then underline examples of the *past continuous* in the paragraph above.**

Past continuous using *while*			
Subject	***be***	**Base + *ing***	**Example sentence**
I, he, she, it	was	making	While I was making dinner, I saw a mouse.
you, we, they	were	studying	The electricity went out while we were studying.

Use the past continuous to talk about events or actions that started in the past and continued for a period of time. To connect two events that happened in the past, use the past continuous with *while* for the longer event. Use the simple past for the shorter event.
Note: You can reverse the two clauses, but you need a comma if *while* comes first.

 Use *while* to combine the sentences below. Read the sentences aloud.

EXAMPLE:
He was sleeping. The phone rang.
While he was sleeping, the phone rang.
Or: ***The phone rang while he was sleeping.***

1. Joshua was painting the cabinet. The shelf fell down.

_____

2. I was brushing my teeth. The water shut off.

_____

3. Fatima saw the crack in the wall. She was hanging a painting.

_____

4. He was taking a shower. The water got cold.

_____

5. The air conditioning broke down. We were eating dinner.

_____

GOAL ▶ Write a letter to your landlord | *Life skill*

A What are some problems tenants have with their landlords? Talk about them with a group. What advice would you give to a new tenant?

B Read the following paragraph about tenants and landlords.

As a tenant, there are many things you need to know to protect yourself. First of all, before you sign the rental agreement, read it very carefully. It may say something that you don't like—for example, it may list restrictions on guests or pets. Also, if you ask your landlord to do something, such as fix a broken toilet, write down when he or she agreed to fix the problem. Then send this in a letter to the landlord. Do this even if you call your landlord or speak to him or her in person. In addition, landlords must keep their buildings clean and in good condition. Remember, it is your right as a tenant to have a comfortable and safe place to live.

C What did you learn about tenants' rights? Write your answers in the space provided.

1. *Read your rental agreement carefully.* _____

2. _____

3. _____

4. _____

D Answer the following questions in a group.

1. What are some other examples of restrictions in a rented house or apartment?
2. How can a landlord keep an apartment clean?
3. How can a landlord keep his or her tenants safe?
4. What things can a landlord do to keep the apartment in good condition?

E　Vu Nguyen had a problem when his family first moved into their new apartment. Read the letter that he wrote to his landlord.

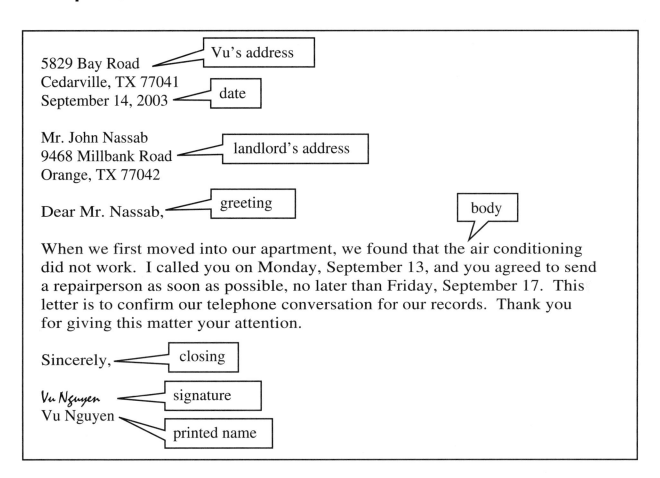

5829 Bay Road — Vu's address
Cedarville, TX 77041
September 14, 2003 — date

Mr. John Nassab
9468 Millbank Road — landlord's address
Orange, TX 77042

Dear Mr. Nassab, — greeting　　　　　　　　　　body

When we first moved into our apartment, we found that the air conditioning did not work. I called you on Monday, September 13, and you agreed to send a repairperson as soon as possible, no later than Friday, September 17. This letter is to confirm our telephone conversation for our records. Thank you for giving this matter your attention.

Sincerely, — closing

Vu Nguyen — signature
Vu Nguyen — printed name

F　What are the different parts of the letter? Discuss them with your teacher.

G　Work with your partner to brainstorm problems you can have in an apartment. Write your ideas below.

EXAMPLE:
The toilet is leaking.

_____

_____

_____

Write a letter to your landlord about a problem that you had in the past or about a current problem. Use Vu's letter on page 53 as an example.

_____ ◀——————— your address

_____

_____ ◀——————— date

_____ ◀——————— landlord's name

_____ ◀——————— landlord's address

_____

_____ ◀——————— greeting

_____

_____

_____

_____

_____

_____

_____

_____

_____

_____ ◀——————— closing

_____ ◀——————— your signature

_____ ◀——————— printed name

I **Read your partner's letter. Check for grammar, spelling, and punctuation.**

 J **Active Task:** Ask your local Housing Authority or use the Internet to find information about tenants' rights.

How much money can we spend?

GOAL ▶ **Make a budget**

Academic skill

A **Listen to Maryanne and Vu talk about their finances. Fill in the missing information.**

Income	
Vu's Salary	$3000
Maryanne's Salary	_____
Total Income	_____
Expenses	
Rent	_____
Utilities	
Electricity	$60
Gas	_____
Telephone	_____ (average)
Other	
Cable TV	$30
Internet	$30
Groceries	_____
Auto	
Gas and maintenance	_____
Car loan	_____
Total Expenses	_____
Extra cash (or cash short)	_____

B **Answer the following questions about the Nguyens' budget with a partner.**

1. What is their income? _____

2. What are their total expenses? _____

3. How much extra cash do they have left after all the bills are paid? (Hint: Subtract total expenses from total income.) _____

4. In your opinion, what are some things they forgot to budget for? _____

    _____

5. What do you think they should do with their extra money? _____

    _____

C Look at the bar graph for the Nguyen family's expenses. Complete the graph with the expenses from the previous page. For this exercise, do not include rent.

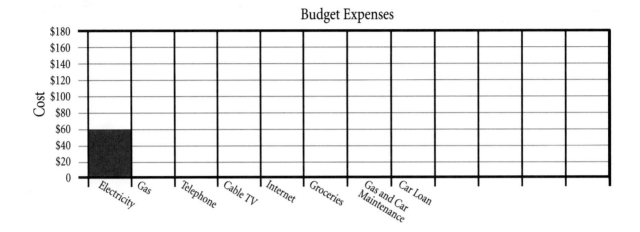

Budget Expenses

D At the bottom of the graph, list the other items the Nguyens should add to their budget. Indicate the budget amount on the graph.

E Active Task: Prepare your own budget and make a bar graph.

Review

A Try this strategy to remember words from the unit.

1. Go back through the unit. Highlight any new words that you want to study.
2. Write each of the words on an index card or a small sheet of paper.
3. Work in pairs. Your partner chooses one card and asks questions to help you guess the word on the card.
4. Switch roles and continue until all the words on the list have been reviewed.

EXAMPLE:
Student A: Who collects the rent? Or: Who owns your apartment?
Student B: tenant
Student A: No, try again.
Student B: landlord
Student A: That's right.

B Read the following classified ad. Rewrite the ad with the full form of the abbreviations.

3 BR w/lge kitchen, 2 car gar,
w/d, new appl., nr. beach
$1500/mo + $500 sec. dep.
Avail 8/30

_____

_____

_____

_____

_____

C Think about your dream home. Write a classified ad that includes everything that you would want. Use abbreviations if you know them.

_____

_____

_____

_____

_____

Review

D You are moving from a house in the country to an apartment in the city. Compare the housing and the environment.

EXAMPLES:
The country has less traffic than the city.
A house has more rooms than an apartment.

_____

_____

_____

_____

E Choose the simple past or the past continuous to complete these sentences.

EXAMPLE:
The lights **went out** (go out) while Maryanne **was taking** (take) a shower.

1. A spider _____ (drop) onto my arm while I _____ (eat) dinner.

2. While Marie _____ (study), the landlord _____ (call).

3. While Terry _____ (clean) the window, he _____ (hurt) his back.

4. Someone _____ (break) into their house while they _____ (visit) friends.

F Imagine you are moving to a new city. What utilities will you have to call and order? Write them below. With a partner, role-play a phone conversation with a customer service representative.

_____   _____   _____

_____   _____   _____

TEAM PROJECT

Create a renter's guide

With a team, you will create a renter's guide that tells people what they need to know before renting an apartment or house.

1. Form a team with four or five students. Choose positions for each member of your team.

Position	Job Description	Student Name
Student 1 Leader	See that everyone speaks English. See that everyone participates.	
Student 2 Secretary	Write information for the guide.	
Student 3 Designer	Design guide layout and add artwork.	
Students 4/5 Assistant(s)	Help secretary and designer with their work.	

2. With your team, decide what will be in your renter's guide.

3. Create the text for your renter's guide.

4. Create artwork for your renter's guide.

5. Present your guide to the class.

PRONUNCIATION

Listen to which words are stressed and choose the correct answer. You will hear each question twice.

1. Are you buying a house?
   a. You are *buying*, not renting.
   b. You are buying a *house*, not a condominium.

2. Are you driving to Florida?
   a. You are *driving*, not flying.
   b. You are going to *Florida*, not California.

LEARNER LOG

In this unit, you learned many things about housing. How comfortable do you feel doing each of the skills listed below? Rate your comfort level on a scale of 1 to 4.

1 = Not so comfortable **2** = Need more practice **3** = Comfortable **4** = Very comfortable

If you circle 1 or 2, write down the page number where you can review this skill.

Life Skill	Comfort Level				Page(s)
I can interpret housing advertisements.	1	2	3	4	_____
I can make decisions about housing preferences.	1	2	3	4	_____
I can identify important information on a rental agreement.	1	2	3	4	_____
I can fill out a rental agreement.	1	2	3	4	_____
I can use the telephone to arrange or cancel utilities.	1	2	3	4	_____
I can interpret utility bills.	1	2	3	4	_____
I can communicate problems to my landlord.	1	2	3	4	_____
I can write a business letter.	1	2	3	4	_____
I can budget household expenses.	1	2	3	4	_____

Grammar

	Comfort Level				Page(s)
I can use comparatives and superlatives.	1	2	3	4	_____
I can use yes/no questions with *do*.	1	2	3	4	_____
I can use the past continuous with *while*.	1	2	3	4	_____

Academic Skill

	Comfort Level				Page(s)
I can make a bar graph.	1	2	3	4	_____

Reflection

1. What was the most useful thing you learned in this unit? _____

_____

2. How will this help you in life? _____

_____

UNIT 4 — Our Community

GOALS

- Use information questions
- Interpret charts and compare information
- Use a chart to make calculations
- Use a telephone directory
- Interpret a map
- Use adverbial time clauses
- Write a paragraph about a place

LESSON 1 **Places in your community**

GOAL ▶ Use information questions | *Grammar*

A Gloria and her family are new to the community. Read her list of Things To Do. Where does she need to go for each one? Listen and write the names of the places below.

Things To Do
a. Find a place for my children to play sports. _____
b. Register for an ESL class. _____
c. Open a checking account. _____
d. Register my car and renew my license. _____
e. Find a place for my children to use computers. _____
f. Pick up some bus schedules. _____

B Practice the following conversation with a partner, using the information above.

> DMV = the Department of Motor Vehicles

Student A: Where can I <u>get a new driver's license</u>?
Student B: At the <u>DMV</u>.

C Study the chart showing how to make information questions.

Information questions			
Location		Where How far What	is the bank? is the school from here? is the address?
Time		When What time How often	does the library open? does the restaurant close? do the trains run?
Cost		How much	does it cost?

D Help Gloria make a list of the questions she needs to ask when she calls. Write questions to match the answers below.

Question	Answer
Ex. What time does the bank open?	The bank opens at 9:00 A.M.
1.	A driver's license costs 25 dollars.
2.	The library is about a mile from here.
3.	The buses run every ten minutes.
4.	You can return books any time.
5.	The DMV is at 112 Main Street.
6.	The children's book section is upstairs.

E On a separate sheet of paper, make your own To Do list like Gloria's on the previous page. Next to each item write the place where you can go in your community and some questions to ask. Look at the example below.

To Do	Place	Question
get information about ESL classes	an adult education program	When do classes start? Where is the school?

F **Active Task:** Go to one of the places on your To Do list and practice asking your questions.

LESSON 2 · Banking choices

A **What is the name of your bank? What kind of bank account do you have? Discuss the following words with your class.**

service fee	direct deposit	unlimited check writing
transactions	minimum balance	ATM teller

B **Riverview Bank offers three kinds of checking accounts. Read the information below.**

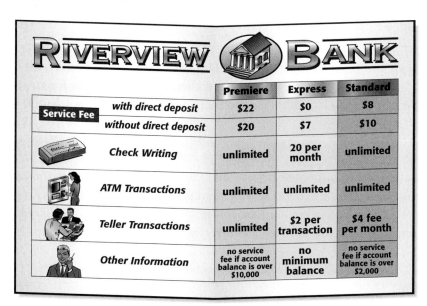

RIVERVIEW 🏦 BANK

		Premiere	Express	Standard
Service Fee	*with direct deposit*	$22	$0	$8
	without direct deposit	$20	$7	$10
Check Writing		unlimited	20 per month	unlimited
ATM Transactions		unlimited	unlimited	unlimited
Teller Transactions		unlimited	$2 per transaction	$4 fee per month
Other Information		no service fee if account balance is over $10,000	no minimum balance	no service fee if account balance is over $2,000

C **With a partner, practice asking the following questions about the information in the brochure.**

EXAMPLE:
Student A: How much is the service fee with direct deposit for the Standard account?
Student B: It's eight dollars.

1. How much is the service fee without direct deposit for the _____ account?

2. How many checks can you write per month with the _____ account?

3. How many ATM transactions can you have per month with the _____ account?

4. How many teller transactions can you have per month with the _____ account? What is the fee for a teller transaction?

D **Read about each of the following people and decide which checking account would be best, using the information in the table on the previous page. Write the account name on the line.**

Do you like using the ATM? Why? Why not?

1. Vu likes to do all of his banking with the ATM. He rarely goes inside the bank. His company deposits his paycheck automatically. He writes about fifteen checks a month. Which account is best for Vu?

_____

2. Michel likes to go inside the bank and do his transactions with a teller. He doesn't trust the ATM and he doesn't like direct deposit. He also writes a lot of checks, so he's looking for an account that allows him unlimited check writing. He likes to keep at least $2,500 in his account. Which account is best for Michel?

_____

3. Gloria and her husband want to buy a new house. They currently have $15,600 in the bank. They pay a lot of bills each month by check, so they want unlimited check writing. Gloria likes to do her banking with a teller. However, her husband works during banking hours and needs to use the ATM. His company deposits his paychecks directly. Which account is best for Gloria and her husband?

_____

E **Write a paragraph about your banking style using the models above. Share your paragraph with another student. Ask him or her to decide which checking account is best for you.**

F **Active Task:** Go to your bank or look on the Internet and get information about different types of accounts.

LESSON 3 The library

GOAL ▶ Use a chart to make calculations

Academic skill

A Do you like to go to your public library? What can you do at a library? Make a list.

_____   _____   _____

_____   _____   _____

B Read the following brochure about library services. You may not understand everything, but see if you can get the general idea.

Library Resources

Circulating materials include hardcover and paperback books, magazines, compact discs, books on tape, and videos. You can check out these circulating materials for three weeks.
Reference materials include newspapers, encyclopedias, atlases, and other nonfiction books. Reference materials can only be used in the library.

Electronic Resources

The library offers a lot of information on computer networks. These networks include U.S. phone listings, reports on publicly traded companies (stocks), and articles from national newspapers. There is no charge to use the Internet.

Information Services

Librarians can help customers find information, use resources, and suggest books for pleasure reading.

Library Cards

If you want to check out materials from the library, you need a library card. Your first card is free. If you lose it, a replacement card costs $2.

Renewing Materials

You can keep materials longer than three weeks if you renew them. You can renew them at the library or over the phone, using your library card.

Fines

If you return materials late or if you lose them, you will have to pay a fine. See the Fine Schedule for more information about lost or overdue materials.

C Read the brochure again and underline the words and phrases that are new to you. Try to guess the meaning of the words using the context. Share your ideas with a partner.

D **Decide if these statements are True or False based on the information you read about the library. Fill in the circle for the correct answer. Then correct each false statement and make it true.**

	True	False
cannot 1. You ~~can~~ check out reference materials.	○	●
2. Librarians can suggest books to read.	○	○
3. You can check out circulating materials.	○	○
4. The library has a database of phone listings from all over the world.	○	○
5. Your first library card costs $2.	○	○
6. You can renew materials over the phone using a driver's license.	○	○
7. You can check out library materials for three weeks.	○	○
8. Circulating materials include books, tapes, videos, and encyclopedias.	○	○
9. If a book is late, it is overdue and you must pay a fine.	○	○
10. There is a fee to use the Internet.	○	○

E **If you want to get a library card, you need to show identification. Put a check next to each item that you have.**

- ☐ driver's license
- ☐ ID card
- ☐ passport
- ☐ rental agreement
- ☐ utility bill
- ☐ rental receipt
- ☐ preprinted checks
- ☐ voter registration

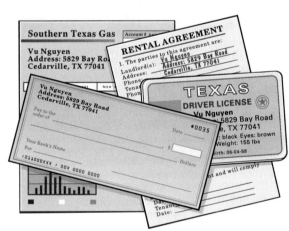

F **Where can you get the items listed above? Discuss your answers with a partner.**

Do you sometimes forget to return a library book? Do you ever lose a book from the library? If so, what happens? Read the information on library fines and losses.

Public Library Fines and Losses	
Overdue Fines	
Hardback Books and Sound Recordings	$.25 per day per item $10 maximum per item
Paperback Books and Magazines	$.25 per day per item $5 maximum per item
Videos	$1 per day per item $20 maximum per item
Lost Materials	
Hardback Books and Audio Recordings	$20
Magazines, Paperbacks, and Pamphlets	$5
Videos/Video case	$55/$4
Books on Tape	$40
Replacement Library Card	$2

 With a partner, read each situation below and determine how much money each person owes the public library. You will need to do some math to answer these questions.

EXAMPLE:

Dinora checked out a paperback book and is returning it 4 days late. How much does she owe? (Answer: $.25 per day × 4 days = $1.00)

1. Jeeva borrowed a video and lost the video, but he still has the case. How much does he owe?

   _____

2. Rochelle borrowed a hardback book and is returning it two months late. How much does she owe? _____

3. Kim Su checked out two bridal magazines to plan her wedding and lost both of them. How much does she owe? _____

4. Steve lost his library card. How much will it cost him to get a new one? _____

5. Carlos borrowed a paperback book and also the book on tape that went along with it. He lost the book and tape. How much does he owe? _____

Active Task: Go to the library and pick up a brochure and a Fines and Losses schedule. Ask for a library card application and fill it out.

GOAL ▶ Use a telephone directory — *Life skill*

A The index of a telephone directory can tell you what pages you need to look at to find information about businesses in your community. Look at part of the index below.

J		**Laser Hair Removal**	707
Janitorial Products–See House Cleaning		**Legal Services**	
Equip & Supls.	624	See Attorneys.	61–111
Jewelry Designers.	697	Bankruptcy Assistance.	240, 241
Job Counseling–See Career & Vocational		Divorce Assistance.	438, 439
Counseling.	294	Libraries–Public.	709
Jugglers–See Clowns.	362	Linens–Retail.	721
		Literacy–See Language Schools.	706, 707
K		Reading Improvement:	
Karate–See Martial Arts Instruction.	749	Instruction and Materials.	1011
Kindergartens–See Schools: Academic,		Lumber–Retail.	738–740
Pre-School & Kindergarten.	1074–1078	Lumber–Used.	740
Kitchen Fixtures–Retail.	701		
Knives–See Cutlery: Retail.	401, 402	**M**	
		Magicians.	740, 741
L		Malls–See Department Stores.	431
Landscape Architects.	703	Gift Shops.	567, 568
Language Interpreters–See Translating &		Shopping Centers & Malls.	1100
Interpreting Services.	1231		

B Read the following information. Using the index above, write the page number where each service can be located.

Ex. For Martin's wedding anniversary, he would like to design a ring for his wife. **697**

1. Eric and Bob want to find a local library to use the computers. _____

2. Angela needs to replace the sheets in her master bedroom. _____

3. Marcia owns a cleaning business and she needs to buy some cleaning products. _____

4. Thomas and Susan are throwing a birthday party for their 10-year-old son. They want some entertainment at the party. _____

C Can you think of some other situations where you would need to use the telephone directory? Make a list with a partner and share your list with the class.

D The first column has questions you could ask when calling a local business. The second column has answers to the questions. Match each question with the correct answer.

Questions

____ 1. How often do the buses run?

____ 2. Where are you located?

____ 3. Do you service Doshina computers?

____ 4. Can I make an appointment?

____ 5. What time do you close?

____ 6. Do you take reservations?

____ 7. Do you sell children's clothes?

____ 8. What are your hours on Sunday?

Answers

a. No, we only sell men's clothing.

b. No, we seat people on a first-come, first-serve basis.

c. We close at 10 P.M.

d. We're open from 10 to 6 on Sunday.

e. What time would you like to come in?

f. We're on the corner of 7th and Pine.

g. They run every 20 minutes.

h. Yes, we service all kinds of computers.

E Complete each of the following conversations with a possible question or answer. When you are finished, practice the conversations with a partner.

Conversation 1

A: Good morning. This is Food Mart.

B: _____

A: We're open now.

B: Great! Thank you.

Conversation 2

A: Thank you for calling The Book Stop. How can I help you?

B: _____

A: Yes, we sell all kinds of books.

B: And what are your hours?

A: _____

B: Thanks!

F With a partner, write a telephone conversation that you might have with a local business. Ask at least two questions in your conversation.

G **Active Task:** Look in the telephone directory for a local restaurant or store. Call the restaurant or store and ask what time it closes.

LESSON 5 Locating places

GOAL ▶ Interpret a map

 Life skill

A **Discuss these questions with your class.**

How far do you live from your school in miles?

What are some major freeways or interstates in your area? What direction do they run?

Where is your school located? What are the nearest towns or cities? What direction are they in relation to your school's location?

B **Gloria and her family lived in Lindon. They decided to move to Victoria, because Victoria has better schools and safer neighborhoods. This is a map of the area where they live. Look at the map. Then answer the questions on the next page.**

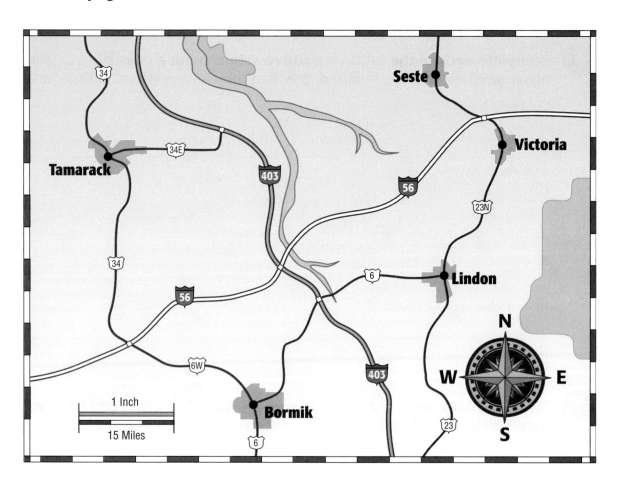

C Work in pairs. Answer the questions below using information from the map. Then ask two more questions of your own.

EXAMPLE:
Student A: Where is Lindon in relation to Victoria?
Student B: <u>Southwest</u>

1. How far is Lindon from Victoria? _____ miles

2. What freeway is Victoria closest to? _____ What direction does this freeway

   run? _____

3. Gloria also considered moving her family to Tamarack. Where is this city located in relation to

   Lindon? _____

4. What direction does Interstate 403 run? _____

5. How far is Bormik from Lindon? _____ miles

6. Where is Bormik located in relation to Lindon? _____

D Study these expressions for giving directions in a city. Can you add any to the list?

Go straight for three blocks.

Turn left. / **Make a** left.

Take 2nd Ave to Oak Street.

It's **next to** the bank.

It's **across from** the park.

It's **on the corner of** First and Main.

_____   _____

_____   _____

_____   _____

E Study the map of Lindon on the next page. Read the directions below to your partner. Your partner will follow the directions on the map.

Student A: Start at the subway on 5th Avenue. Take a right out of the subway. Turn left on Main Street. Go straight for four blocks. Take a left on 1st Avenue. It's on the corner of Oak and First Avenue. What's the name of the building? _____

Student B: Start at the post office on Main Street. Turn right out of the post office. Turn left on 3rd Avenue. Go straight for two blocks. It's on the corner of Maple Street and 3rd Avenue. What's the name of the building? _____

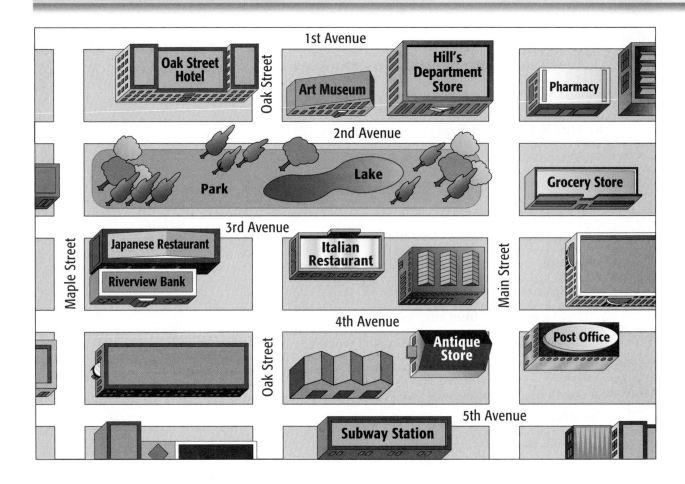

F Give your partner directions to different places on the map. Start your conversations using the questions below. Then ask directions for other places on the map.

How can I get to	Hill's Department Store	from	Riverview Bank?
	the pharmacy		Oak Street Hotel
	the subway station		the post office
	the Art Museum		the Japanese restaurant

G **Active Task:** Use a road atlas or use a map locator on the Internet to get driving directions from your home to your school.

GOAL ▶ **Use adverbial time clauses**

Grammar

A **Look at the picture and read about Gloria's busy day.**

Yesterday was a busy day! After I woke up, I got the kids ready for school. Before my husband left for work, I ironed his shirt. When everyone left the house, I made my list of errands and off I went. First, I returned some books to the library. I stopped by the bank to make a deposit after I returned the books. Then I went to the post office to mail a package to my family back in Brazil. The next errand on my list was grocery shopping. But before I went grocery shopping, I remembered to go to the cleaners and pick up some skirts. And finally, when I finished shopping, I went home. It was a long morning!

B **Put the things that Gloria did in the correct order.**

____ picked up dry cleaning

____ got the kids ready for school

____ ironed her husband's shirt

____ husband and kids left the house

____ made deposit at the bank

_1_ woke up

____ made a list of errands

____ mailed a package at the post office

____ returned books to the library

____ went back home

____ went grocery shopping

Study the chart with your teacher.

| Adverbial clauses with *before, after, when* ||
Example	**Rule**
After I returned the books, I stopped by the bank to make a deposit.	The action closest to *after* happened first. (First, she returned the books. Second, she went to the bank)
Before I went grocery shopping, I stopped by the cleaners to pick up some skirts.	The action closest to *before* happened second. (First, she went to the cleaners. Second, she went grocery shopping.)
When everyone left the house, I made my list of errands and went out.	The action closest to *when* is completed and the next action begins. (First, everyone left. Second, she made her list.)
I went home *when* I finished shopping. *When* I finished shopping, I went home.	You can reverse the two clauses and the meaning stays the same. You need a comma if the adverbial clause goes first.

D **In each of the following sentences, underline the action that happened first.**

EXAMPLE:

After <u>I woke up</u>, I made breakfast.

1. I stopped by the bank to make a deposit **before** I returned the books.
2. **Before** Wendy went shopping, she went to the gym.
3. **When** my kids came home, I made dinner.
4. Eddie read the paper **before** he went to work.

E **Write sentences with adverbial clauses, following the example below. Then rewrite the sentence, reversing the clauses.**

EXAMPLE:

(1) Ali finished work. (when) (2) He went out with his friends.

    a. *__When Ali finished work, he went out with friends.__*

    b. *__Ali went out with his friends when he finished work.__*

1. (1) Yasu saved enough money. (before) (2) He bought a new bicycle.

    a. _____

    b. _____

2. (1) The alarm went off. (after) (2) Maya jumped out of bed.

    a. _____

    b. _____

GOAL ▶ **Write a paragraph about a place**

Academic skill

A **Gloria is writing a paragraph about Victoria. Read her notes below.**

Reasons I love Victoria

safe neighborhoods (kids play in park)   affordable housing (can buy new house)

good schools (nationally recognized)   ~~good shopping~~

~~fair weather (never gets too cold)~~   good job opportunities (computer industry)

B **Gloria decided to focus on a few ideas for her paragraph. She wrote six sentences, but they are not in the correct order. Choose the best *topic sentence* and write *1* in front of it. Choose the best *conclusion sentence* and write *6* in front of it. Then choose the order of the *support sentences* and number them *2–5*. (Look at page 6 to review the different parts of a paragraph.)**

____ Thanks to the great job market in Victoria, my husband got an excellent position in a computer company.

____ Our family can buy a nice house because the housing prices are very affordable here.

____ I love Victoria so much that I can't imagine moving.

____ The neighborhoods are very safe, so I can let my children play in the park with other children.

____ The excellent schools in this area are nationally recognized.

____ There are many reasons I love my new hometown, Victoria.

C **On a separate sheet of paper, write Gloria's sentences as a paragraph. Use transitions to connect your support ideas.**

| First of all, | Second of all, | Furthermore, | First, |
| Second, | Also, | Third, | Finally, |

Now write about your town. Follow each step below.

1. Write the name of your town or city. _____

2. Brainstorm at least six reasons why you love (or don't like) your town.
   EXAMPLE: ***friendly people***

   a. _____

   b. _____

   c. _____

   d. _____

   e. _____

   f. _____

3. Circle the four most important reasons.

4. Write a topic sentence for your paragraph.

   _____

5. Write four support sentences based on the four reasons you chose above.

   a. _____

   _____

   b. _____

   _____

   c. _____

   _____

   d. _____

   _____

6. Write a conclusion sentence.

   _____

 On a separate sheet of paper, write a paragraph about your town or city, using the information above. Use transitions to connect your ideas.

Review

A Here are some words from this unit. Write them in alphabetical order in your notebook. Then look up the words in your dictionary to see if you were correct. Write sentences to help you remember the most difficult words.

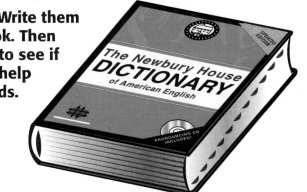

transaction	reserve
teller	replacement
restaurant	register
receipt	schedule
reference	renew

B Work with a partner. How many things can you do at the library? Make a list below, using the new vocabulary from Lesson 3.

EXAMPLE:
Use the Internet.

_____

_____

_____

C You are visiting a new city. You want to take the bus from your hotel to go to a restaurant. Call the bus company and the restaurant. What questions will you ask? Write your questions below. Then role-play a conversation with a partner.

EXAMPLE:
Where is the bus stop?

_____

_____

_____

_____

_____

D **Write sentences with adverbial clauses, following the example below. Use** ***before, after,*** **or** ***when.***

EXAMPLE:
I woke up. I made breakfast.
After I woke up, I made breakfast.

1. The children finished breakfast. I got them ready for school.

_____

2. I got some money out of the ATM. I bought some groceries.

_____

3. Mala finished work. She went to the movies.

_____

4. Luigi graduated from college. He got a job in a computer company.

_____

E **Draw a map showing the way from your school to a nearby restaurant. Then** **write the directions. Read them to your partner and see if your partner can** **draw the map.**

Draw your map here: Write your directions here:

_____

_____

_____

_____

_____

_____

_____

_____

_____

_____

_____

TEAM PROJECT

Create a community brochure

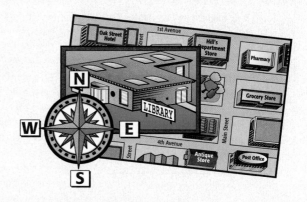

With a team, you will create a brochure about your community.

1. Form a team with four or five students. Choose positions for each member of your team.

Position	Job Description	Student Name
Student 1 Leader	See that everyone speaks English. See that everyone participates.	
Student 2 Secretary	Write information for the brochure.	
Student 3 Designer	Design brochure layout and add artwork.	
Students 4/5 Assistant(s)	Help secretary and designer with their work.	

2. Imagine that a new family has moved into your neighborhood and you want to tell them all about your community. With your team, make a list of everything you want to include in your community brochure, such as information about the library, banks, and other local services.

3. Create the text for your community brochure. (You may give each member of the team responsibility for one section of the brochure.)

4. Create artwork for your community brochure.

5. Present your brochure to the class.

PRONUNCIATION

We use stress to make important words clearer. Listen and repeat. Then try to make your own examples.

1. A: Is it about **fifty** miles?   B: No, it's **fifteen** miles.
2. A: Is it number **thirty**-three?   B: No, it's number **forty**-three.
3. A: Is your house on Wilson **Avenue**?   B: No, it's on Wilson **Street**.
4. A: Do you open at **7**A.M.?   B: No, we open at **7:30** A.M.

LEARNER LOG

In this unit, you learned many things about community. How comfortable do you feel doing each of the skills listed below? Rate your comfort level on a scale of 1 to 4.

1 = Not so comfortable **2** = Need more practice **3** = Comfortable **4** = Very comfortable
If you circle 1 or 2, write down the page number where you can review this skill.

Life Skill	Comfort Level				Page(s)
I can identify resources in a community.	1	2	3	4	_____
I can compare information about bank services.	1	2	3	4	_____
I can interpret a table about library fines.	1	2	3	4	_____
I can use a telephone directory to find services.	1	2	3	4	_____
I can use the telephone to get basic information.	1	2	3	4	_____
I can interpret maps.	1	2	3	4	_____
I can give and receive directions.	1	2	3	4	_____
I can indicate order of schedule or plans.	1	2	3	4	_____

Grammar					
I can use information questions.	1	2	3	4	_____
I can use adverbial time clauses with *when, before,* and *after.*	1	2	3	4	_____

Academic Skill					
I can interpret information about library services.	1	2	3	4	_____
I can write about my community.	1	2	3	4	_____

Reflection

1. What was the most useful thing you learned in this unit? _____

_____

2. How will this help you in life? _____

_____

Health

GOALS

- Identify parts of the body
- Use the present perfect
- Fill out a medical history form
- Use the future conditional
- Interpret food labels
- Interpret dietary information
- Interpret an article about fitness

Call the doctor

GOAL ▶ Identify parts of the body

Vocabulary

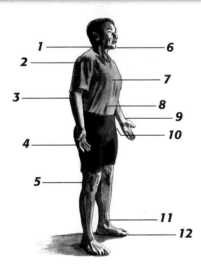

wrist	ankle
hip	knee
neck	chest
stomach	finger
shoulder	toe
elbow	chin

A Label the parts of the human body, using the words from the box.

1. ___*neck*___
2. _____
3. _____
4. _____
5. _____
6. _____
7. _____
8. _____
9. _____
10. _____
11. _____
12. _____

B What other parts of the body can you name? Work with a partner. Label other parts of the body you know by drawing a line from the body and writing the name.

Match the doctor with the specialization. Ask your teacher to help with answers and pronunciation. Write your answers in the chart below. Add one more to the list.

Doctor	Specialization
_c_ 1. podiatrist	a. allergies and asthma
_____ 2. dermatologist	b. children
_____ 3. gynecologist/obstetrician	c. feet
_____ 4. cardiologist	d. teeth
_____ 5. ophthalmologist	e. mental illness
_____ 6. pediatrician	f. heart
_____ 7. dentist	g. eyes
_____ 8. allergist	h. women and childbirth
_____ 9. psychiatrist	i. skin
_j_ 10. _____	j. _____

D **Use the statements below to make a recommendation about which doctor to see.**

EXAMPLE:
Student A: My mother's feet hurt.
Student B: She should see a podiatrist.

1. My mother's feet hurt.	6. I feel depressed.
2. My father is worried about his heart.	7. I have a rash on my neck.
3. My six-year-old son has a fever.	8. I think I have a cavity.
4. My nose is running and my eyes are itchy.	9. My sister thinks she is pregnant.
5. My eyes hurt when I read.	10. _____

E **Active Task:** Use the phone book. Look up *physicians* to find a list of doctors and their specializations. Which ones are in your area?

 **Illnesses and symptoms**

| GOAL ▶ Use the present perfect | *Grammar* |

 A Read the conversation and answer the questions.

Doctor: What seems to be the problem?
Hanif: I have a terrible backache.
Doctor: I see. How long have you had this backache?
Hanif: I've had it for about a week.
Doctor: Since last Monday?
Hanif: Yes, that's right.

1. What is the matter with Hanif? _____

2. When did his problem start? _____

B Make similar conversations using the information below.

EXAMPLES:
Student A: What's the matter?
Student B: I feel dizzy.
Student A: How long have you felt dizzy?
Student B: For two days.

Student A: What's the matter?
Student B: My back hurts.
Student A: How long has your back hurt?
Student B: Since yesterday.

1. I have a headache. (for five hours)
2. My eyes are red. (since last night)
3. My shoulder hurts. (for two weeks)
4. I feel tired. (since Monday)
5. My throat is sore. (for three days)

Base	Past participle
be	been
have	had
feel	felt
hurt	hurt

GOAL ▶ **Use the present perfect**

C **Study the chart with your teacher.**

Present perfect					
Subject	*have*	**Past participle**		**Length of time**	**Example sentence**
I, you, we, they	have	been	sick	since Tuesday	I *have been* sick since Tuesday.
she, he, it	has	had	a backache	for two weeks	She *has had* a backache for two weeks.
Use the present perfect for events starting in the past and continuing up to the present.					

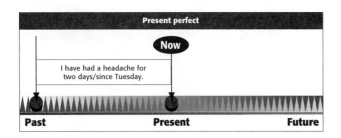

Period of time	**Point in time**
for . . .	since . . .
. . . five minutes	. . . last night
. . . three days	. . . Thursday
. . . one week	. . . November
. . . two years	. . . 1998
. . . a long time	. . . I was a child

D **Make sentences using the present perfect and *for* or *since*.**

EXAMPLE:

Ali has a backache / Monday

Ali has had a backache since Monday.

1. I have a cold / three days

_____

2. My leg hurts / last night

_____

3. Julie feels dizzy / one week

_____

4. Julio and Karel are sick / two weeks

_____

E **Work in pairs. Role-play a conversation between a doctor and a patient. Choose an illness and ask questions about the symptoms. Use *how long* and the present perfect.**

GOAL ▶ **Fill out a medical history form** **Vocabulary**

 A Look at the illustration of the internal parts of the human body. Review the pronunciation of new words with your teacher.

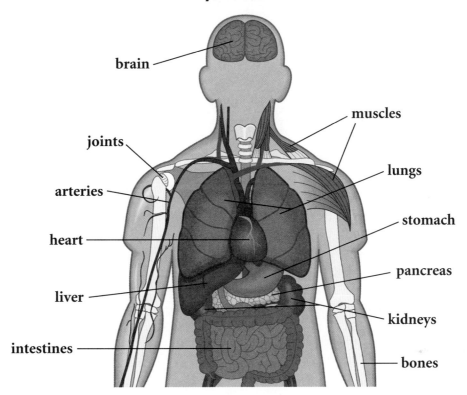

brain

muscles

joints

lungs

arteries

stomach

heart

pancreas

liver

kidneys

intestines

bones

B Can you talk to your doctor about your medical history? Write the part of the body next to the correct condition or disease. Then compare your answers with a partner. Add one idea of your own.

Condition or disease	Part of body
_b_ 1. high blood pressure	a. brain
____ 2. asthma	b. heart and arteries
____ 3. ulcers	c. joints
____ 4. stroke	d. stomach
____ 5. arthritis	e. lungs
_f_ 6. _____	f. _____

GOAL ▶ Fill out a medical history form

C Imagine that you are at a health clinic for a stomachache that you have had for five days. Fill out the medical history form below. For this exercise, make up the personal information.

MEDICAL HISTORY FORM

1. Do you have or have you ever had:

Patient   Family Member

Yes	No	Yes	
☐	☐	☐	High Blood Pressure/Heart Attack
☐	☐	☐	Diabetes/Kidney Disease
☐	☐	☐	Asthma/Lung Disease
☐	☐	☐	Seizures
☐	☐	☐	Stomach Problems
☐	☐	☐	Arthritis
☐	☐	☐	Other Illnesses or Infectious Diseases
☐	☐	☐	Major Surgery/Hospitalization/Injury

If yes, please list:_____

2. Are you sensitive or allergic to any drugs?   Yes_____   No_____
   If yes, please list:_____
3. Are you under the care of a physician now?   Yes_____   No_____
   Physician's Name:_____
4. Do you wish a copy of your visit sent to your physician?   Yes_____   No_____
5. Are you taking any medications now or recently?   Yes_____   No_____
   If yes, please list:_____
6. Describe your current problem:_____

D **Active Task:** Find information about a medical condition that is common in your family. Use the Internet or a health encyclopedia. What kind of information can you find?

LESSON 4 Effects of health habits

A Read the chart below and match each health habit to an effect. There may be more than one answer. Compare answers with a partner.

Cause	Effect
_j_ 1. are very stressed	a. have healthy lungs
___ 2. drink too much alcohol	b. not be well-rested
___ 3. stay in the sun too long	c. harm your liver
___ 4. eat junk food every day	d. not have strong bones
___ 5. exercise at least three times a week	e. get lung cancer
___ 6. don't eat enough calcium	f. protect your skin
___ 7. don't sleep eight hours every night	g. get skin cancer
___ 8. smoke cigarettes	h. be fit and healthy
___ 9. stay away from smoking	i. gain weight
___ 10. wear sunscreen	j. have high blood pressure

B Study the chart with your teacher.

Future conditional statements	
Cause—*if* + present tense	***Effect—future tense***
If you *are* very stressed,	you *will have* high blood pressure.
If you *don't eat* enough calcium,	you *won't have* strong bones.

We can connect a cause and an effect by using a *future conditional* statement. The *if*-clause (or the *cause*) is in the present tense and the *effect* is in the future tense.

Effect—future tense	**Cause—*if* + present tense**
You *will have* high blood pressure	*if* you *are* very stressed.

You can reverse the clauses, but use a comma only when the *if*-clause comes first.

C With a partner, practice making conditional statements with the information from exercise A. Try to use different subjects *(I, you, we, they, he, she)*.

1. _____

2. _____

3. _____

4. _____

D Complete the following sentences with the correct form of the verbs in parentheses.

EXAMPLE:

If you **wash** (wash) your hands a few times a day, you **won't get** (not get) so many colds.

1. If Anh _____ (get) her teeth cleaned regularly, she _____ (not have) so many cavities.

2. My dad _____ (not lose) weight if he _____ (keep) eating foods that are high in fat.

3. My skin _____ (burn) if I _____ (not put) sunscreen on it.

4. If people _____ (not stretch) before they exercise, they _____ (have) sore muscles.

5. If you _____ (drink) too much beer, you _____ (get) a big stomach.

6. If Susan _____ (not eat) before she runs her race, she _____ (pass out).

7. Araceli _____ (lose) the weight she gained when she was pregnant if she _____ (walk) with her baby every day.

8. Bang Vu _____ (not be able to) talk tomorrow if he _____ (not rest) his voice.

E Write four future conditional statements about health habits you would like to have. Then read them to your partner.

EXAMPLE:

If I get more sleep, I will concentrate better on my work.

1. _____

2. _____

3. _____

4. _____

Nutrition labels

GOAL ▶ **Interpret food labels**

 A Read the nutrition label for macaroni and cheese.

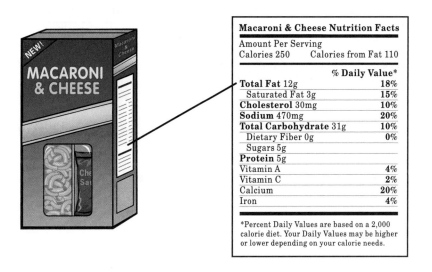

Macaroni & Cheese Nutrition Facts

Amount Per Serving
Calories 250   Calories from Fat 110

	% Daily Value*
Total Fat 12g	18%
Saturated Fat 3g	15%
Cholesterol 30mg	10%
Sodium 470mg	20%
Total Carbohydrate 31g	10%
Dietary Fiber 0g	0%
Sugars 5g	
Protein 5g	
Vitamin A	4%
Vitamin C	2%
Calcium	20%
Iron	4%

*Percent Daily Values are based on a 2,000 calorie diet. Your Daily Values may be higher or lower depending on your calorie needs.

  B Listen to Darla explain nutritional information to her grandmother. Listen to both parts of the conversation before you do the following exercise.

 C Listen to each part of the conversation again and answer the questions below. Fill in the circle next to the correct answer. Then share your answers with a partner.

Part 1

1. What does Grandma need to look at if she wants to watch her salt intake?
   ○ sodium   ○ saturated fat

2. How many servings are in this box of Macaroni and Cheese?
   ○ two   ○ four

3. How many calories should an average adult have each day?
   ○ 200   ○ 2000

Part 2

1. What should Grandma avoid for a healthy heart?
   ○ cholesterol and saturated fat
   ○ carbohydrates and saturated fat

2. What should a diabetic look for on a food label?
   ○ sugar   ○ salt

3. What nutrient helps digestion?
   ○ iron   ○ fiber

4. What nutrient is good for bones?
   ○ calcium   ○ vitamin A

D **Read the nutritional guide below.**

Recommended Amount of Calories and Fat a Day		
Calories per day 2000	Saturated fat in grams 20 or less	Total fat in grams 65

Quick Guide to % Daily Value for Nutrients (sodium, protein, vitamins, calcium, iron)*

5% or less is LOW   20% or more is HIGH

*Percent Daily Values are based on a 2,000 calorie diet. Your Daily Values may be higher or lower depending on your calorie needs.

E **Now look at the macaroni and cheese label on the previous page. Answer the questions below with a partner.**

1. How much fat does the macaroni and cheese contain? Is it high in fat?
2. How much sodium does it contain? Is it high in sodium?
3. Does it contain any protein? How much?
4. What vitamins does it contain? Is it high in vitamins?
5. Is the macaroni and cheese a good source of calcium?
6. Do you think the macaroni and cheese is a healthy food choice? Explain your answers.

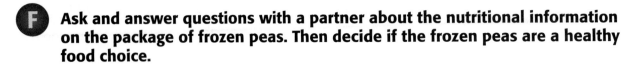

Frozen Peas Nutrition Facts	Amount/Serving	%DV*
Ingredients: Green peas, Salt Serving size 2/3 cup (87g) Servings Per Container About 5	Total Carbohydrate 12g	4%
	Fiber 4g	16%
	Sugars 6g	
Calories 70 Calories from Fat 5	Protein 5g	
	Vitamin A	6%
Total Fat 0.5g — 1%	Vitamin C	15%
Sat. Fat 0g — 0%	Calcium 0%	0%
Cholesterol 0mg — 0%	Iron 4%	4%
Sodium 100mg — 4%	*Percent Daily Values are based on a 2,000 calorie diet. Your Daily Values may be higher or lower depending on your calorie needs.	

F **Ask and answer questions with a partner about the nutritional information on the package of frozen peas. Then decide if the frozen peas are a healthy food choice.**

EXAMPLE:
Student A: How many calories are in one serving?
Student B: 70 calories.

 G **Active Task:** Look at some nutrition labels on food products you have at home or look them up on the Internet. Share the information with your class.

LESSON 6 — A healthy diet

GOAL ▶ **Interpret dietary information**

A The food pyramid will help you make good decisions about daily food choices. Look at the number of servings carefully. Then answer the questions below.

Food Guide Pyramid
A Guide to Daily Food Choices

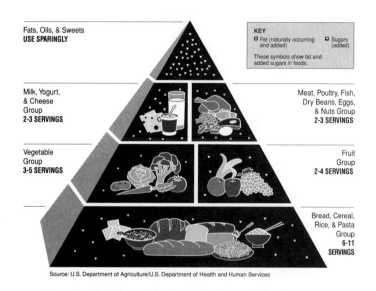

Source: U.S. Department of Agriculture/U.S. Department of Health and Human Services

1. Which foods should you eat the most of? _____

2. Which foods should you eat the least of? _____

3. How many servings of fruit should you eat every day? _____ How many do you eat? _____

4. How many servings of vegetables should you eat every day? _____ How many do you eat? _____

5. What are some examples of sweets? _____

   _____

B Work with a partner and plan three meals according to the food pyramid. Compare your meal plans with another pair's plan. Whose menu is the most delicious and nutritious?

Breakfast	Lunch	Dinner

Read the dietary guidelines below.

Aim for Fitness	Build a Healthy Base	Choose Sensibly
• Aim for a healthy weight. • Be physically active each day.	• Let the pyramid guide your food choices. • Choose a variety of grains daily, especially whole grains. • Choose a variety of fruits and vegetables daily. • Keep foods safe to eat.	• Choose a diet that is low in saturated fat and cholesterol and moderate in total fat. • Choose beverages and foods to moderate your intake of sugars. • Choose and prepare foods with less salt. • If you drink alcoholic beverages, do so in moderation.

Source: Dietary Guidelines for Americans 2000, Center for Nutritional Policy and Promotion, USDA

D **Discuss the following questions in a group.**

1. What are some different ways to stay physically active?
2. Do you eat a low fat diet?
3. Does your diet contain a lot of salt and sugar?
4. What do you think drinking alcoholic beverages in moderation means?
5. According to the dietary guidelines, how good are your eating habits?

E **The dietary guidelines give you general information. Read the specific tips about healthy eating. Put a check mark ✓ next to tips you follow or would like to follow. Then discuss your answers with a partner.**

Tips for healthy eating	Follow	Would like to follow
Ex. Eat fresh fruit every day.		✓
1. Keep raw vegetables in the refrigerator to eat as a snack.		
2. Eat a variety of foods so you get all the nutrients you need.		
3. Eat lean meats like fish and chicken.		
4. Choose fat free or low fat dairy products.		
5. Try not to drink beverages with a lot of sugar, like soft drinks.		
6. Flavor foods with herbs and spices instead of salt.		
7. Pay attention to serving sizes.		
8. Choose foods that have less saturated fat.		

F Have you ever gotten sick from something you ate? What did you eat? Why do you think you got sick? Tell your story to a group.

G Match the pictures and the sentences below. Write the correct letter next to each sentence.

a.    c.    e.

b.    d. 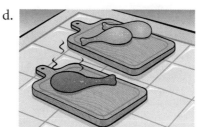   f.

___*f*___ 1. Clean. Clean and wash hands and surfaces often.

_____ 2. Separate. Separate raw, cooked, and ready-to-eat foods while shopping, preparing, or storing.

_____ 3. Cook. Cook foods to a safe temperature.

_____ 4. Chill. Refrigerate perishable food promptly.

_____ 5. Serve safely. Keep hot food hot.

_____ 6. Check and follow the label.

H Write this sentence in your own words: "When in doubt, throw it out."

_____

LESSON 7 Healthy living

GOAL ▶ Interpret an article about fitness

Academic skill

A You are going to read part of an article about physical fitness. Before you read, write one piece of advice which you think the article will contain. Then read the article.

_____

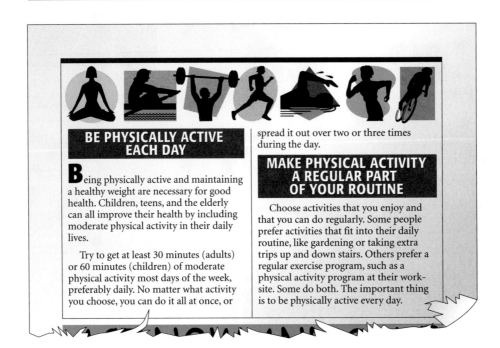

BE PHYSICALLY ACTIVE EACH DAY

Being physically active and maintaining a healthy weight are necessary for good health. Children, teens, and the elderly can all improve their health by including moderate physical activity in their daily lives.

Try to get at least 30 minutes (adults) or 60 minutes (children) of moderate physical activity most days of the week, preferably daily. No matter what activity you choose, you can do it all at once, or spread it out over two or three times during the day.

MAKE PHYSICAL ACTIVITY A REGULAR PART OF YOUR ROUTINE

Choose activities that you enjoy and that you can do regularly. Some people prefer activities that fit into their daily routine, like gardening or taking extra trips up and down stairs. Others prefer a regular exercise program, such as a physical activity program at their work-site. Some do both. The important thing is to be physically active every day.

B Are these sentences true or false? Fill in the circle under the correct answer.

	True	False
1. Physical exercise is necessary for good health.	○	○
2. Elderly people do not need to exercise.	○	○
3. You should do all your exercise at one time.	○	○
4. Maintaining a healthy weight is not important, as long as you exercise.	○	○
5. Climbing stairs is a good way to exercise regularly.	○	○
6. The most important thing is to exercise regularly.	○	○

C Discuss these questions with your partner.

1. Do you exercise more or less than recommended in the article? _____

2. Does your worksite offer physical activity programs? What are they? _____

_____

D Look at the examples of physical activities. Which is an example of a routine activity? Which is an example of a recreational activity?

Anna plays tennis twice a week with her friend.

Mike rides his bicycle to the office every day.

E Read the list of routine activities. Put a ✓ next to activities you have tried. Put an *x* next to activities you would like to try. Add two more activities to the list. Compare your answers with a partner.

❑ Walk or ride a bike to work.
❑ Walk up stairs instead of taking an elevator.
❑ Get off the bus a few stops early and walk the remaining distance.
❑ Garden.
❑ Push a stroller.

❑ Clean the house.
❑ Play actively with children.
❑ Take a brisk 10-minute walk or bike ride in the morning, at lunch, and after dinner.
❑ _____
❑ _____

F Read the list of recreational activities. Put a ✓ next to activities you have tried. Put an *x* next to activities you would like to try. Add two more activities to the list. Compare your answers with a partner.

❑ Walk, jog, or bicycle.
❑ Swim or do water aerobics.
❑ Play tennis or racquetball.
❑ Golf (pull cart or carry clubs).
❑ Canoe.
❑ Cross-country ski.

❑ Play basketball.
❑ Dance.
❑ Take part in an exercise program at work, home, school, or gym.
❑ _____
❑ _____

Read the article. Then answer the questions below with a partner.

HEALTH BENEFITS OF PHYSICAL ACTIVITY

Being physically active for at least 30 minutes on most days of the week reduces the risk of developing or dying of heart disease. It has other benefits as well. No one is too young or too old to enjoy the benefits of regular physical activity. Two types of physical activity are especially beneficial:

(1) Aerobic activities

These are activities that speed your heart rate and breathing. They help cardiovascular fitness.

(2) Activities for strength and flexibility

Developing strength may help build and maintain your bones. Carrying groceries and lifting weights are two strength-building activities. Gentle stretching, dancing, or yoga can increase flexibility. ■

1. Why is it important to be physically active?
2. Why are aerobic activities good for you?
3. What are some examples of aerobic activities?
4. What are some examples of strength-building activities?
5. What types of activities can increase your flexibility?
6. What are some activities you do for strength and flexibility?

H **Read about some more benefits of physical activity. Then discuss the questions with a partner.**

• Increases physical fitness • Helps build and maintain healthy bones, muscles, and joints • Builds endurance and muscular strength • Lowers risk factors for cardiovascular disease, colon cancer, and Type 2 diabetes	• Helps manage weight • Helps control blood pressure • Promotes psychological well-being and self-esteem • Reduces feelings of depression and anxiety

1. What diseases can exercise help prevent?
2. How does exercise help your circulatory system?
3. How does exercise affect your mood and your mental health?
4. What are some other benefits of exercise?

  Active Task: Find a web site for a health club or go to a local gym. What classes are offered there? Make a list of the types of classes you would like to try.

Review

A Look at the list of vocabulary from this unit. Write each word under the correct category. Use a dictionary to check your answers.

ankle	ophthalmologist	dentist	worry	itchy	sore	sprain
stay	hospital	tired	cough	diabetes	stress	protect	gain
dry	cholesterol	healthy	safe	prepare	gentle	stretch

Noun	Verb	Adjective
ophthalmologist	worry	itchy

B Match each condition with the doctor who treats it. Then have a conversation with your partner using the model below.

EXAMPLE:
Student A: My skin is very red and itchy. What should I do?
Student B: You should see a dermatologist.

Condition	Doctor
____ 1. My skin is very red and itchy.	a. dentist
____ 2. My heart is beating quickly.	b. dermatologist
____ 3. My husband is always sneezing.	c. gynecologist/obstetrician
____ 4. My baby is coughing.	d. cardiologist
____ 5. My mother's toe hurts.	e. pediatrician
____ 6. There is something in my eye.	f. ophthalmologist
____ 7. My brother has a cavity.	g. podiatrist
____ 8. I feel nervous all the time.	h. allergist
____ 9. My sister is pregnant.	i. psychiatrist

C Make sentences using the present perfect and *for* or *since*.

EXAMPLE:

Ali has a backache / Monday

Ali has had a backache since Monday.

1. My neck hurts / two days

_____

2. Maria feels dizzy / yesterday

_____

3. My children have a cold / Friday

_____

4. Peter is sick / two weeks

_____

5. I have an earache / 10:00 A.M.

_____

6. They are absent from work / one month

_____

D Complete the following sentences, using the future conditional.

1. If you eat out every night, _____.

2. _____ if he goes to the best doctors in the country.

3. If _____, they will look and feel great.

4. If Paulo smokes a pack of cigarettes a day, _____.

5. If _____, you will get sick.

6. If _____, you will improve your flexibility.

7. If you read nutrition labels, _____.

8. If _____, you will have a lot of cavities.

T E A M
P R O J E C T

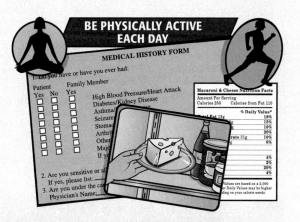

Create a healthy living plan

With a team, you will create a healthy living plan.

1. Form a team with four or five students. Choose positions for each member of your team.

Position	Job Description	Student Name
Student 1 Leader	See that everyone speaks English. See that everyone participates.	
Student 2 Secretary	Write information for the plan.	
Student 3 Designer	Design plan layout and add artwork.	
Students 4/5 Assistant(s)	Help secretary and designer with their work.	

2. Make a list of all the information you want to include, such as diet and exercise.

3. Create the different sections of your healthy living plan, such as a guide to reading nutrition labels, a guide to exercise, doctors and their specializations, and common symptoms and diseases.

4. Add artwork to the plan, such as maps to find parks and gyms in your area or drawings of the food pyramid.

5. Prepare a table of contents.

6. Present your plan to the class.

PRONUNCIATION

Listen to each word. Which syllable is stressed? Follow the example below.

• • ● • •

| ophthalmologist | cardiologist | dermatologist | gynecologist |

| psychiatrist | dentist | pediatrician | optician |

LEARNER LOG

In this unit, you learned many things about health. How comfortable do you feel doing each of the skills listed below? Rate your comfort level on a scale of 1 to 4.

1 = Not so comfortable **2** = Need more practice **3** = Comfortable **4** = Very comfortable

If you circle 1 or 2, write down the page number where you can review this skill.

Life Skill	Comfort Level				Page(s)
I can identify parts of the body.	1	2	3	4	_____
I can identify doctors and their specializations.	1	2	3	4	_____
I can recognize common medical conditions.	1	2	3	4	_____
I can fill out a medical history form.	1	2	3	4	_____
I can interpret food labels.	1	2	3	4	_____
I can interpret a table on dietary guidelines.	1	2	3	4	_____
I can talk about food safety.	1	2	3	4	_____

Grammar					
I can use the present perfect.	1	2	3	4	_____
I can use time expressions with *since* and *for*.	1	2	3	4	_____
I can use future conditionals to express cause and effect.	1	2	3	4	_____

Academic Skill					
I can interpret an article on physical fitness.	1	2	3	4	_____

Reflection

1. What was the most useful thing you learned in this unit? _____

_____

2. How will this help you in life? _____

_____

UNIT 6

Getting Hired

GOALS
- Identify job titles and skills
- Use infinitives and gerunds
- Interpret job advertisements
- Fill out a job application
- Write a letter of application
- Discuss interview skills
- Answer interview questions

LESSON 1 Jobs and careers

GOAL ▶ Identify job titles and skills | *Vocabulary*

A Look at the pictures and write the correct letter next to each job title below.

a.

b.

c.

d.
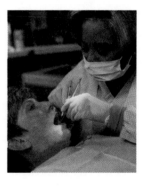

_____ 1. Graphic artist

_____ 2. Home health aide

_____ 3. Dental hygienist

_____ 4. Bookkeeper

B Which job is most interesting? Which job is most difficult? Why?

C **Match the job with the description.**

_e_ 1. graphic artist   a. cleans teeth

____ 2. repair technician   b. takes care of children

____ 3. administrative assistant   c. designs and maintains yards

____ 4. dental hygienist   d. writes programs for computers

____ 5. landscaper   e. designs artwork for companies

____ 6. bookkeeper   f. types, files, and does general office work

____ 7. home health aide   g. uses equipment in a factory or on a construction site

____ 8. computer programmer   h. keeps financial records

____ 9. nanny   i. fixes appliances and equipment

____ 10. machine operator   j. takes care of sick people in their own homes

D **Practice the following conversation with a partner. Use the information above.**

EXAMPLE:
Student A: What does a graphic artist do?
Student B: A graphic artist designs artwork for companies.

E **Work with a partner. Think of four more jobs and write what each person does.**

EXAMPLE:
A postal worker delivers mail.

1. _____

2. _____

3. _____

4. _____

F **Active Task:** Ask your family and friends about different positions and job titles in their workplaces.

LESSON 2 Job skills and preferences

GOAL ▶ **Use infinitives and gerunds** *Grammar*

A **What are your special job skills? Put a check next to the things you are good at. Add any skills that are not on the list.**

❑ answer phones and take messages

❑ assemble things

❑ cook

❑ draw

❑ drive a car or truck

❑ fix machines

❑ order supplies

❑ balance accounts

❑ operate machines

❑ talk to customers

❑ read maps

❑ sew

❑ speak other languages

❑ take care of children

❑ take care of the elderly

❑ type

❑ repair computers

❑ use computers

❑ _____

❑ _____

B **Are there any skills you want to improve? Are there any skills you want to learn? List them below.**

_____

_____

C **Exchange lists with a partner. Can you think of ways your partner can learn or practice those skills? Use ideas from the box below to give your partner advice.**

EXAMPLE:

Student A: I want to learn to take care of the elderly.

Student B: Maybe you can volunteer at a hospital or nursing home.

volunteer	ask a friend to teach you	practice at home
take a class	find a job training program	get trained at your company

D Claude needs a job. Can you suggest a good job for him?

Claude is quiet and shy. He is friendly, but he doesn't really like to talk to customers. He is very good at assembling things. When he was a teenager, he enjoyed fixing bicycles. He likes to be busy. He wants to get a job where he can use his technical skills.

E Study the chart with your teacher. Then underline examples of infinitives and gerunds in the paragraph above.

Infinitives and gerunds (Infinitive = *to* + verb Gerund = verb + *ing*)			
Verb	**Followed by**	**Example sentence**	**Other similar verbs**
want	infinitive	He wants *to get* a job.	plan, decide
enjoy	gerund	He enjoys *fixing* bicycles.	finish, give up
like	either	He likes *to talk*. / He likes *talking*.	love, hate

F Are these verbs followed by an infinitive, a gerund, or either? Fill in the circle next to the correct answer.

	infinitive	gerund	either
EXAMPLE: I like _____ on a team.	○ to work	○ working	● to work/working
1. I enjoy _____ problems.	○ to solve	○ solving	○ to solve/solving
2. I want _____ to customers.	○ to talk	○ talking	○ to talk/talking
3. I decided _____ math.	○ to study	○ studying	○ to study/studying
4. I hate _____ decisions.	○ to make	○ making	○ to make/making
5. I gave up _____ two years ago.	○ to smoke	○ smoking	○ to smoke/smoking
6. I love _____ machines.	○ to repair	○ repairing	○ to repair/repairing

G **What are your special job skills? Put a check next to the things you are good at. Add any skills that are not on the list.**

❑ solve problems   ❑ work with my hands

❑ work under pressure   ❑ help people

❑ work in a fast-paced environment   ❑ organize information

❑ work on a team   ❑ work with money

❑ make decisions   ❑ talk to customers

❑ pay attention to details   ❑ read and follow directions

❑ _____   ❑ _____

H **Study the chart below.**

Gerunds after prepositions					
Subject	**Verb**	**Adjective**	**Preposition**	**Gerund / Noun**	**Example sentence**
I	am	good	at	calculating	I am good at *calculating*.
she	is	interested	in	math	She is interested in *math*.

A gerund or a noun follows an adjective + a preposition. Some other examples of
adjectives + prepositions are: *afraid of, tired of, bad at, worried about.*

I **Tell your partner about your skills and interests. What things are you good at, bad at, interested in, tired of, and afraid of? Your partner will suggest a good job for you.**

EXAMPLE:
Student A: I am good at paying attention to details. I'm interested in organizing information.
Student B: Maybe you should be a bookkeeper.

J **Write a paragraph about your job skills on a separate sheet of paper. What are you good at? What are you interested in learning? How do you plan to learn or practice these skills?**

K **Active Task:** Go to your local library or career center. Locate books on finding the right career. Tell the class about one title.

GOAL ▶ Interpret job advertisements   *Life skill*

A Read the following job advertisements.

24 NewsObserver   Sunday, October I

HELP WANTED

❶ Auto technician: Do you like to work on cars? Do you have an excellent attitude, good mechanical skills, & the ability to learn fast? Strong electronics background preferred. Call Chrissy at (310) 555-9078.

❹ Photographer. Reliable? Enjoy children? Join our team taking school pictures. A cheerful personality is a plus. We offer paid training. Must have car & proof of insurance. Fax resume to Lifetouch Studios 318-555-7440.

❼ Need caring, **Licensed Nurse's Aide** to care for elderly couple. Housing on site. Competitive salary. Send resume with references to: P.O. Box 2728 Morgan City, LA 70381.

❷ Acme Construction, **Administrative Assistant.** Min. 2 yrs. exp in clerical. Good computer skills req. Ability to work under pressure and type 40wpm. Fax res. 818-555-3141.

❺ Fast-growing supermarket chain seeks bright, motivated **managers** for meat & produce. Prior management experience, required. Excellent salary and benefits. Fax resume to: 626-555-1342.

❽ Dependable **custodian** for 3 apartment buildings. Min. 2 yrs exp. plumbing, carpentry, painting, repair. Must have own tools and car $12-14/hr+benes 818-555-3500x523.

❸ **Receptionist,** weekends: 10am-6pm. Requires HS diploma (or equiv) and 1 year experience. Excellent phone & organizational skills along with a pleasant attitude a must! Please apply in person to: 396 Marcasel Avenue, Los Angeles, CA 90066.

❻ Detail-oriented **pharmacy clerk** needed to process insurance forms & assist customer. Must be biling/Spanish. Strong commun & org skills. Great bene. Call: Armine (626) 555-6613.

WA

B Are there any words or abbreviations that are new to you? List them below and discuss them with your teacher.

_____   _____   _____

_____   _____   _____

C **Read the ads again and answer the questions below.**

1. What experience should the auto technician have? **_electronics background_**

2. Which employer wants someone who can work under a lot of pressure? _____

3. Which job provides training? _____

4. Which job requires references? _____

5. Which jobs require a friendly personality? _____

6. Which jobs require a car? _____

7. Which job requires someone who likes details? _____

8. Which job requires someone who is bilingual? _____

9. What job offers housing? _____

10. What are some ways to apply for these jobs? (e.g. fax resume) _____

D **Read each of the following descriptions and decide which job or jobs the person should apply for. Write the job titles in the spaces provided.**

1. Lance recently moved here and needs to find a job. At his old job, he answered the phone, typed letters, and filed paperwork. He would like a job doing the same thing. What jobs should he apply for?

   _____

2. Kyung was recently laid off from his janitorial job at the local school district. He had been working there for ten years and took care of all the maintenance and repairs for the school. What job should he apply for?

   _____

3. Kim has two children and wants to work while they are in school. She doesn't have any clerical skills, but she is cheerful and friendly. What job should she apply for?

   _____

4. Rita manages a bakery but wants to find a job closer to home. She is smart and willing to work hard. She really likes to work with people and would like to find a job in the same line of work. What job should she apply for?

   _____

E **Which of the jobs do you like best? Why?**

 F **Active Task:** Find classified ads on the Internet or in the newspaper. Choose three jobs that you would like.

GOAL ▶ **Fill out a job application**

 A **Look at the ways people apply for jobs. How did you get your last job? What's the best way to get a job? Discuss your answers with a partner.**

- Personal connection (You knew someone at the company.)

- Went to an employment agency

- Replied to a classified ad

- Saw a *Help Wanted* sign and filled out an application

- Introduced yourself to a manager and filled out an application

- Sent a resume to a company

B **Not every business advertises available positions. If you want to work somewhere, go in and ask for an application. Read the conversation below.**

Ramona: Excuse me. May I speak to the manager please?

Employee: She's not here right now. Can I help you?

Ramona: Are you hiring now?

Employee: As a matter of fact, we are.

Ramona: What positions are you hiring for?

Employee: We need a *manicurist* and a *receptionist*.

Ramona: Great. Can I have an application, please?

Employee: Here you go. You can drop it off any time.

Ramona: Thanks a lot.

Employee: Sure. Good luck.

C **Practice the conversation above. Fill in your own job titles.**

D You will have to write information about previous employers on a job application. Think about a job you had before. Fill out the information as best you can.

Previous Employer			
Date Month and Year	Name and Address of Employer	Salary	Position
From:			
To:			
Duties performed:			
References			
Supervisor's name		Phone Number	May we contact?

E Read the *Rules for Filling Out an Application.* What words might fit in the blanks? Then listen and fill in the missing words.

Rules for Filling Out an Application

1. Use a _____ _____ — blue or _____ ink.

2. Don't _____ _____ any mistakes. Use correction fluid to _____ any mistakes.

3. Answer every _____. If the question doesn't apply to you, put _____ (not applicable).

4. Tell the _____! Never _____ on your job application.

5. Don't _____ or wrinkle the application.

6. Keep the application _____— no food or coffee stains!

7. Write as _____ as possible. _____ it if you can.

8. If you don't _____ the question, ask someone before you answer it.

F **Active Task:** Go out into your community and get a job application. Fill out the application for practice.

GOAL ▶ Write a letter of application

 Read about Ramona Garza.

Ramona Garza is looking for work as a receptionist. She recently left her job because she wanted to make more money. She saw an ad in the paper for a hair salon that was hiring receptionists. She got an application and filled it out. She is ready to turn in her application, but she wants to write a letter of application to go along with it.

B **Read Ramona's letter of application.**

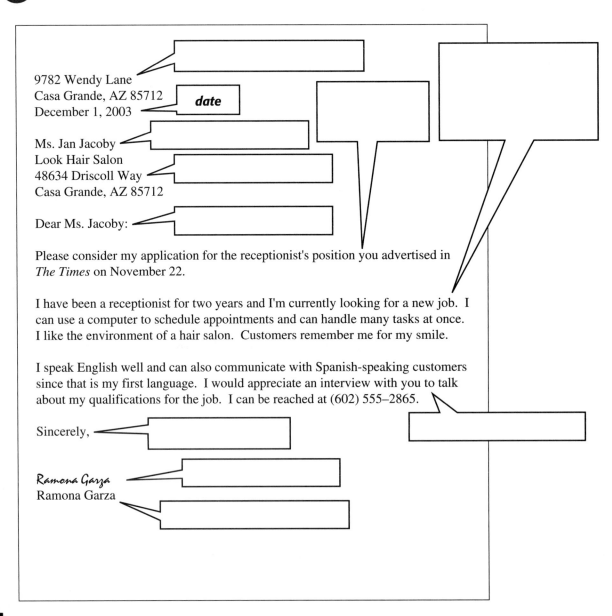

9782 Wendy Lane
Casa Grande, AZ 85712
December 1, 2003 — *date*

Ms. Jan Jacoby
Look Hair Salon
48634 Driscoll Way
Casa Grande, AZ 85712

Dear Ms. Jacoby:

Please consider my application for the receptionist's position you advertised in *The Times* on November 22.

I have been a receptionist for two years and I'm currently looking for a new job. I can use a computer to schedule appointments and can handle many tasks at once. I like the environment of a hair salon. Customers remember me for my smile.

I speak English well and can also communicate with Spanish-speaking customers since that is my first language. I would appreciate an interview with you to talk about my qualifications for the job. I can be reached at (602) 555–2865.

Sincerely,

Ramona Garza
Ramona Garza

C **Read the list of items that are included in a letter of application.**

- date
- name of contact person
- signature
- reason for writing
- reasons you are qualified for the job
- company's address

- formal closing
- printed name
- formal greeting
- your address
- request to meet with the employer

D **Label the letter of application on page 110 with the items listed above. The date has been done for you.**

E **Imagine you are applying for a job you found in the newspaper on page 106. Answer the questions below.**

1. What is the job title? _____

2. How did you learn about the job? _____

_____

3. What are your skills for this job? _____

_____

_____

_____

F **Practice writing a letter of application using information about yourself. Use Ramona's letter as an example. Make sure you include everything in the list above.**

GOAL ▶ Discuss interview skills

A Have you ever had a job interview? What happened? Tell your partner.

B During a job interview, an employer will try to find out about an applicant's character and personality. Listen to the recording and find three character traits which employers look for. Then read the paragraphs below to check your answers.

Your job interview is the most important part of the application process. This is when the employer gets to meet you and learn more about you. Employers are interested in your skills and experience, but they also look for personality and character traits.

Do you stand tall and smile confidently? Employers will notice your self-confidence. Managers want to hire employees who have confidence in themselves and will have confidence in the job they are doing.

Do you like to work hard and do a good job? Another important thing an interviewer looks for is enthusiasm about work. People who are enthusiastic about a job make great employees. They are happy with the work and usually stay with the company for a while.

Are you friendly and easy to talk to? Do you pay attention to how other people are feeling? Warmth and sensitivity are also very important traits. A person with these characteristics will make a good co-worker, someone who can work well with others.

Do you have some or all of these traits? Can you show that you have these traits in an interview? If the answer is yes, you will have a good chance of getting the job.

C Discuss the following questions with a partner.

1. In your opinion, which is the most important: confidence, enthusiasm, or a friendly personality?

2. According to the reading, how can you use body language to show you are confident? Can you think of any other ways you can show confidence through body language?

3. How can you show an employer that you are enthusiastic about the job and the company?

4. According to the reading, why do employers like to hire warm, sensitive people?

5. Do you think there are other character traits that employers like? What are they?

D With your classmates, discuss what kind of clothing and accessories are appropriate or not appropriate for a job interview. Fill in your responses in the chart. Use the words from the box and add some of your own ideas.

Clothing and Appearance for Interviews

Men	Appropriate	Not appropriate
	long-sleeved shirt	*T-shirt*

Women	Appropriate	Not appropriate

earrings

tattoos

make-up

sneakers

tie

jewelry

pants

suit

belt

shorts

cuff links

dress

handbag

briefcase

jacket

T-shirt

long hair

jeans

nail polish

E **Active Task:** At home, put together an appropriate interview outfit. Try it on and see how professional you look!

LESSON **7** Why do you want to work here?

| GOAL ▶ | Answer interview questions | *Life skill* |

 Imagine you are preparing for a job interview. What will you talk about in the interview? Choose a job from the classified ads on page 106 or choose one of your own. Read the sample interview questions and fill in the chart below.

1. What are your skills?

> *I can type 60 wpm.*
> _____
> _____

2. Why do you think you would be good at this job?

> *I have two years' experience.*
> _____
> _____

3. How would you describe your personality?

> _____
> _____
> _____

4. What did you like and dislike about your last job?

> _____
> _____
> _____

5. Do you have any questions?

> _____
> _____
> _____

B Answer these additional interview questions.

1. Would you rather work full-time or part-time? _____

2. What hours can you work? _____

3. Are you willing to travel to other locations? _____

4. How would you get to work? _____

5. What salary do you expect? _____

6. Can you get recommendations from your previous employers? _____

C Study the chart below.

would rather					
Subject	*would rather*	**Base**	*than*	**Base**	**Example sentence**
I, you, she, he, it, we, they	would ('d) rather	work alone	than	work with people	I *would rather* work alone than work with people.

Note: You can omit the second verb if it is the same as the first verb.
Ex. I would rather work nights than (work) days.

D Which work situation do you prefer? Talk to your partner about your preferences.

EXAMPLE:
Student A: Would you rather work inside or outside?
Student B: I'd rather work inside because I hate the cold.

1. work alone / in a team
2. work days / nights
3. get paid by the hour / weekly

4. have your own business / work for someone else
5. retire at 65 / work till you are 70
6. have a male supervisor / a female supervisor

E Write two sentences about your ideal work situation.

EXAMPLE:
I'd rather work on a team than alone because I like talking to people.

1. _____

2. _____

F Imagine you are an employer interviewing someone for a job as an administrative assistant in a very busy doctor's office.

1. Make a list of six character traits you would look for. Use words from the box.

honest	confident	funny	friendly	sensitive
warm	enthusiastic	arrogant	motivated	thoughtful
helpful	careful	intelligent	cheerful	reliable

a. _____ d. _____

b. _____ e. _____

c. _____ f. _____

2. What skills does an administrative assistant need to have? List them below.

EXAMPLE: _**Phone skills**_

_____

_____

_____

3. Prepare six questions to ask in the interview.

a. _____

b. _____

c. _____

d. _____

e. _____

f. _____

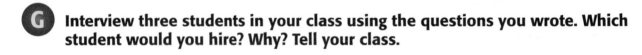

G Interview three students in your class using the questions you wrote. Which student would you hire? Why? Tell your class.

 H **Active Task:** Use the Internet or go to the library to find interview tips. Find a good book or web site and tell the class.

Review

A Look up the following words in the dictionary. Write them on the lines and mark the correct syllable stress.

1. applicant   `applicant _____`

2. previous   _____

3. bookkeeper   _____

4. technician   _____

5. computer   _____

6. equipment   _____

7. environment   _____

8. require   _____

B Complete these sentences using a gerund or an infinitive form of the verb in parentheses.

1. I like _____ on a team. (work)

2. I am good at _____ to customers. (talk)

3. They hate _____ the phone. (answer)

4. I decided _____ computers next semester. (study)

5. He is interested in _____ cars. (repair)

6. We finished _____ our reports yesterday. (write)

C Imagine that a friend has a job interview. Give him or her advice about what he or she should or shouldn't wear. How can your friend appear professional?

EXAMPLE:
You should wear a suit. You shouldn't wear a T-shirt.

_____

_____

_____

_____

_____

D **What would you rather do? Think about the things you don't like about your current job. Write four sentences using *would rather* to express your preferences.**

1. _____

2. _____

3. _____

4. _____

E **What kind of personality should people have for these jobs? Write two adjectives for each job. Share your answers with a partner.**

EXAMPLE:

Home health aide: ***reliable, sensitive***

1. Manager in a clothing store: _____

2. Receptionist in a dentist's office: _____

3. Nanny: _____

4. Custodian in a school: _____

5. Teacher: _____

F **Write six interview questions for one of the following jobs. Interview a partner, using the questions.**

landscaper	receptionist	furniture store manager	bookkeeper
computer technician	waiter	assembler in a factory	home health aide

EXAMPLE:

Can you type?

_____

_____

_____

_____

_____

_____

T E A M
P R O J E C T

Create a job application portfolio

With your team, you will plan the contents and layout for a job application portfolio. Each individual will create his or her own job application portfolio.

What does a job application portfolio include?	
• a job application information sheet • a list of rules for filling out a job application • a sample application letter • sample interview questions and answers • certificates	• awards • transcripts • performance reviews • letters of recommendation

1. Form a team with four or five students. Choose positions for each member of your team.

Position	Job Description	Student Name
Student 1 Leader	See that everyone speaks English. See that everyone participates.	
Student 2 Secretary	Write a list for the job application portfolio.	
Student 3 Designer	Design layout and order of job application portfolio.	
Students 4/5 Assistant(s)	Help secretary and designer with their work.	

2. Make a list of all the information you want to include in your portfolio. Look at the list above for help. Decide how many pages you will need.

3. With your team, decide the best order for your portfolio.

4. Individually, collect and create items to put in your portfolio. Put your portfolio together.

5. Share your portfolio with at least two other students.

6. Set up an interview with your teacher and share your portfolio with him or her.

PRONUNCIATION

Intonation (the way your voice goes up or down) can tell a lot about your personality or your mood. Listen to these speakers and decide which word describes their intonation.

friendly   bored   kind   impatient   confident   enthusiastic

Speaker 1: _____   Speaker 3: _____   Speaker 5: _____

Speaker 2: _____   Speaker 4: _____   Speaker 6: _____

LEARNER LOG

In this unit, you learned many things about getting hired. How comfortable do you feel doing each of the skills listed below? Rate your comfort level on a scale of 1 to 4.

1 = Not so comfortable **2** = Need more practice **3** = Comfortable **4** = Very comfortable

If you circle 1 or 2, write down the page number where you can review this skill.

Life Skill	Comfort Level	Page(s)
I can identify job titles and qualifications.	1 2 3 4	_____
I can describe my job skills.	1 2 3 4	_____
I can interpret job advertisements.	1 2 3 4	_____
I can fill out a job application.	1 2 3 4	_____
I can write a letter of application.	1 2 3 4	_____
I know what is appropriate to wear to an interview.	1 2 3 4	_____
I can answer interview questions.	1 2 3 4	_____

Grammar

I can use infinitives and gerunds.	1 2 3 4	_____

Academic Skill

I can read about and discuss interviewing skills.	1 2 3 4	_____
I can write a letter of application.	1 2 3 4	_____

Reflection

1. What was the most useful thing you learned in this unit? _____

_____

2. How will this help you in life? _____

_____

UNIT 7

On the Job

GOALS

- Identify good employee behavior
- Use possessive pronouns and adjectives
- Interpret a pay stub
- Discuss benefits
- Use modals *could* and *might*
- Communicate at work
- Write a work journal

LESSON 1 **Attitudes at work**

GOAL ▶ Identify good employee behavior | *Life skill*

A Listen to the two employees talk about their jobs. What does Leticia do? What does So do?

B With a partner, write some examples of Leticia's and So's behavior on a separate sheet of paper.

C In your opinion, who is the better employee? Why? Can you think of other examples of good and bad employee behavior?

Leticia: I think an ideal manager should be demanding.
Ellen: I agree. A manager shouldn't be too easygoing.

D **What is an ideal manager like? What are ideal co-workers like? Use the adjectives from the box below to have a conversation with your partner.**

friendly	courteous	funny	serious	demanding	respectful
strict	quiet	interesting	ambitious	hardworking	patient
relaxed	intelligent	easygoing	lazy	opinionated	reserved

E **Answer the questions about relationships at work with a partner.**

1. Do you think it's important to be friends with your co-workers? Why or why not?
2. Do you think it's important to be friends with your manager? Why or why not?

LESSON 2 Relationships at work

| GOAL ▶ Use possessive pronouns and adjectives | *Grammar* |

 A Read the conversation below. Which words are possessive *adjectives* and which words are possessive *pronouns?*

Ellen: *My* boss is quite demanding and she always wants *her* reports on time.
Leticia: Yes, *your* manager is more demanding than *mine.*
Ellen: Yeah, and *yours* is friendlier.

 B Study the chart. Which possessive pronouns have an *s* at the end? Which possessive adjective and possessive pronoun are the same?

Possessive adjectives and possessive pronouns			
Possessive adjectives	my your his her our their	*Possessive adjectives* show possession of an object and come before the noun.	This is *her* office.
Possessive pronouns	mine yours his hers ours theirs	*Possessive pronouns* show possession of an object and act as a noun.	This office is *hers.*

 C Underline the possessive adjective in each sentence. Circle the possessive pronoun.

EXAMPLE:

My sister's manager is generous. But my manager is more generous than hers.

1. Their job is boring. But our job is more boring than theirs.

2. My two cousins work at the supermarket. Their job is hard. But our jobs are harder than theirs.

3. My husband gets a good salary. His salary is better than mine.

4. My brother says his co-workers are friendly. But my co-workers are friendlier than his.

5. I like her manager, but mine is much more easygoing.

6. His office is clean but ours is bigger.

D **Circle the correct word in each sentence below.**

EXAMPLE:
She keeps (her)/hers workspace very clean.

1. She never eats at (her/hers) desk, but they always eat at (they/theirs).

2. That office is (you/yours).

3. Did you give them (your/yours) time card?

4. (They/Their) company has more employees than his.

5. That's (your/yours) book. Where is (my/mine) book?

6. We will give you (our/ours) proposal, so you can compare it with (your/yours).

E **Make groups of three or four students. Compare your jobs. (Being a student or a homemaker are jobs too! If you are retired, talk about the job you had.) Then write four sentences about your group, using possessive pronouns.**

EXAMPLE:
Anita has a friendly manager. But Juan's manager is friendlier than hers.

_____

_____

_____

_____

F **What makes you happy in a job? Write *1* next to the thing that is most important to you. Write *8* next to the thing that is the least important. Then compare answers with a partner.**

____ salary   ____ a good relationship with my manager

____ location   ____ a good relationship with co-workers

____ hours   ____ opportunities for promotion

____ interesting work   ____ opportunities to learn new skills

| GOAL ▶ | Interpret a pay stub | Life skill |

A Discuss the following vocabulary with your teacher.

year-to-date	marital status	rate of pay	earnings
Medicare	Social Security	federal tax	net pay
state disability	gross pay	payroll end date	tax deductions
401K	pre-tax deductions	retirement	state tax

B Look at Leticia's pay stub. Then answer the questions below.

1.

Employee Name: Leticia Rosales	Marital Status: Single
Check Number: 0768	Payroll Begin/End Dates:
SS Number: XXX–XX–XXXX	5/14/02–5/27/02

Hours and Earnings			
Description	Rate of Pay	Hours/Units	Earnings
Hourly/Day/Monthly	14.75	80	1,180.00

2.

Tax Deductions		
Tax Description	Current Amount	Calendar Year-to-Date
Federal	102.78	205.56
State	19.72	39.44
Social Security	10.68	21.36
Medicare	14.29	28.58
State Disability		

3.

Pre-Tax Deductions	
Description	Amount
401k	50.00
Current Total	50.00
Year-to-Date Total	100.00

4.

	Gross Pay	Pre-Tax Deductions	Pre-Tax Retirement	Tax deductions	Net Pay
Current	1,180.00	50.00		147.47	982.53

C Where can you find this information in the pay stub? Write the number of each section.

1 EXAMPLE: weeks the paycheck covers

____ total amount she takes home   ____ information about taxes

____ information about retirement savings   ____ hourly wage

D **Answer the following questions about Leticia's pay stub.**

1. Did she pay into Social Security this month? If so, how much? _____

2. Does she contribute any money to a retirement account? If so, how much? _____

3. Does she pay into Medicare? _____

4. Does she pay state disability insurance? _____

5. How many hours did she work in the past two weeks? _____

6. How much federal tax has she paid this year? _____

7. How much money did she make this month after taxes? _____

8. How much money did she make this month before taxes? _____

9. How much state tax did she pay this month? _____

10. Is she married? _____

11. What does she get paid per hour? _____

12. How much money in pre-tax deductions has she contributed this year? _____

E **Discuss the following questions with a partner.**

1. Would you rather get paid every week, twice a month, or once a month? Why?
2. Would you rather get paid a salary or get paid by the hour? Why?

F **Active Task:** Look at your pay stub and figure out how much you pay in taxes.

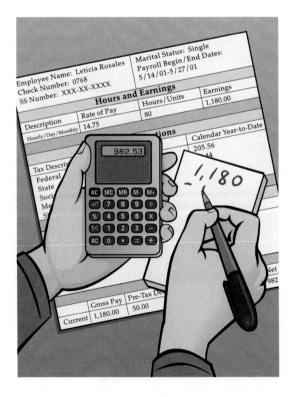

LESSON 4 What are the benefits?

GOAL ▶ **Discuss benefits** | *Life skill*

A Read the following list of benefits. Put a check next to the ones at your present or last job or your friend's job.

- ❑ 401K
- ❑ bonus
- ❑ dental insurance
- ❑ disability insurance
- ❑ family leave
- ❑ health insurance
- ❑ daycare

- ❑ maternity leave
- ❑ medical leave
- ❑ overtime
- ❑ paid personal days
- ❑ paid sick days
- ❑ paid vacation days
- ❑ _____

B Benefits are extra things that a company offers its employees in addition to a salary. Listen to the career counselor talk about the benefits that three companies offer. Put the information that you hear into the chart below.

Company name	Health/dental insurance	Sick days	Vacation days	401K
Set It Up Technology	full medical and dental insurance			yes—$1 for every dollar you contribute
Machine Works				
Lino's Ristorante				yes—50 cents for every dollar you contribute

C Which company would you rather work for? Why? Discuss your answer with a partner.

D **Complete each of the following statements with a word from exercise A.**

1. **_Disability insurance_** is for people who get injured at work.

2. You take a _____ when you stay home because you don't feel well.

3. Most companies are required to offer their employees _____ to take care of them and their families when they are sick.

4. Some companies offer a retirement plan called a _____.

5. When a company shares its profits with the employees, each employee gets a

   _____.

6. When a woman has a new baby, she is allowed to take _____.

7. When you take a day off to do something for yourself, it is called a _____.

8. When you work longer than you are required to, you should get paid _____.

E **With a group, imagine that you are starting a new company and you have to decide what benefits you will offer. Answer the questions below.**

1. How many sick days will each employee receive? _____

2. How many personal days will you give each employee? _____

3. How many vacation days will each employee get? _____

4. Will you offer overtime pay? If yes, how much will you pay employees for overtime work?

   _____

5. What other benefits will you offer your employees? List them below.

   _____

   _____

  Active Task: Choose a company you know or would like to work for. Use the Internet or contact their human resources department to find out what benefits they offer.

GOAL ▶ Use modals *could* and *might*　　　　*Grammar*

A **Look at the pictures below. What type of job does each person have? What health and safety issues should they consider?**

Minh

Arnie

Wassim

Robin

B **Write the name of the person who should wear each of the items below.**

1. a back support belt _____

2. safety goggles _____

3. earplugs _____

4. a hairnet _____

C **Ask your partner if he or she has to wear safety items at work.**

D   **Read the conversation between Arnie and his manager, Fred. Do you think Fred is right?**

Fred: Arnie, why aren't you wearing a back support belt?

Arnie: Oh, I don't need one.

Fred: If you don't wear a belt, you might hurt your back.

Arnie: I don't think so. I'm really careful.

Fred: I know but you could fall. Or you might lift something that is too heavy.

Arnie: You're right. If I get hurt, I might miss work. I could lose a lot of money if I can't work.

Fred: Exactly. Let me get you a belt.

 E   **Underline *might* and *could* in the conversation above. Circle the verb that comes after each modal. Then study the chart below.**

Modal Verbs - *could* and *might*			
Subject	**Modal**	**Base verb**	**Example sentence**
I, you, he, she,	could	fall	You could fall.
it, we, they	might	miss	I might miss work.

We use the modals *might* and *could* to say that there is a chance that something will happen in the future.

 F   **We also use *might* and *could* in conditional sentences with *if* when we are talking about possibilities. Complete the following sentences.**

EXAMPLE:
If Arnie doesn't wear a back support belt, he could hurt his back.

1. If Minh forgets to tie her hair back, _____.

2. Jose _____ if he doesn't wear a hard hat.

3. Wassim _____ if he doesn't wear safety goggles.

4. Vanessa might damage her hearing if she _____.

5. If Lilly doesn't buckle her seatbelt, she _____.

6. If Paolo doesn't wear a dust mask, _____

   _____.

G Look at the safety hazards below. What's wrong in each picture?

1.

3.

2.

4.

H Write sentences about what could and might happen in the situations above.

1. _____

_____

2. _____

_____

3. _____

_____

4. _____

_____

I What does your employer or school do to keep your workplace safe? Tell the class.

  J **Active Task:** Do you wear safety equipment at work? Use the Internet or check the telephone directory to find out where you can buy safety equipment.

GOAL ▶ **Communicate at work**

A **Identify the different types of communication. Write *compliment* or *criticism* next to each sentence below.**

EXAMPLE:
Good job! *compliment*

1. You need to work a little faster. _____

2. You shouldn't wear that shirt to work. _____

3. That was an excellent presentation. _____

4. You are really friendly to the customers. _____

5. Please don't take such long breaks. _____

6. You are one of our best workers. _____

 B **Are these people responding to a compliment or a criticism? Write *compliment* or *criticism* next to each sentence below. Then listen and check your answers.**

1. Thanks. I'm glad to hear it. _____

2. I'll try to do better next time. _____

3. It's nice of you to say so. _____

4. I'm sorry. I won't wear it again. _____

5. I appreciate you telling me that. _____

6. Okay. It won't happen again. _____

C **Use the sentences above to make conversations with a partner.**

EXAMPLE:
Student A: Good job!
Student B: Thank you. I did my best.

Compare these two conversations. Then study the charts.

Conversation 1:
Employee: Excuse me. Would you mind looking over this report for me before I send it out?
Manager: Yes, of course. That's no problem.

Conversation 2:
Susan: Could you give me a hand with this box?
Co-worker: Sure, I'll be right over.

Polite requests	
Would you mind helping me?	Polite and formal
Could you help me, *please*?	Polite and friendly
Can you give me a hand?	Polite and informal
Come here!	Very informal, or impolite

	Agree	Refuse
Sure.	No problem.	No. I'm really sorry.
That's fine.	Certainly.	I'm sorry, but I can't.
Of course.		I'd like to, but I can't because . . .

When we speak to friends or colleagues, it is polite to be less formal. When we speak to a boss or a manager, it is polite to be more formal.

  Listen to these people talking to their bosses, co-workers, and employees. Are they being impolite or polite? Check the correct answer.

1. ___ impolite   ___ polite   3. ___ impolite   ___ polite

2. ___ impolite   ___ polite   4. ___ impolite   ___ polite

 Work with a partner. Practice making and responding to polite requests.

1. Ask your taller co-worker to reach a box on a high shelf.
2. Ask your co-worker to give you a ride home.
3. Ask your employee to make a photocopy.
4. Ask your boss to help you check some accounts.

GOAL ▶ **Write a work journal**   *Life skill*

A **Read about Alexander.**

My name is Alexander, and I'm a childcare worker at
Grow Me Up Childcare. All of the childcare workers keep
work journals. It's a requirement to receive our paychecks.
This journal describes what we do during the day, what kids
we interact with, and any problems we might have. The
owner likes to read our journals once a week to see what we
did and to know what children we were interacting with. It's
good for her to know when she is talking to the parents.

I usually put my daily schedule in my journal. I also write
a description of everything I did that day. It takes me about
15 minutes each day to write in my journal. I like to go back
and read my journal. It's amazing how quickly I forget what
I've done!

B **Answer the questions below. Then share your answers with a partner.**

1. What does a work journal describe? _____

2. Why does Alexander keep a work journal? _____

_____

3. Who reads Alexander's work journal? _____

4. What does Alexander write in his journal? _____

5. How long does it take Alexander to write in his journal? _____

6. Do you keep a journal of any kind? If you do, what do you write in your journal?

_____

C **Read Alexander's work journal.**

Date: September 26

6:55 am	Arrive/sign in	12:30-1:10 pm	Make lunch and clean up
7:00-8:30	Parents drop children off	1:15-2:30	Naptime/quiet play
8:30-10:15	Children play indoors	2:30-3:00	Story time
10:15	Snack time	3:15-5:00	Field trip
10:30-12:00	Teach pre-school activities	5:00-6:00	Parents pick children up

Today I arrived at the day care center at 6:55 a.m. After I signed in, I helped check the children in as their parents dropped them off. After all the children arrived, I took care of a group of children during indoor playtime. It was an exciting day because Ethan L., who is usually very shy, sang the whole alphabet to me! At 12:30 pm I helped to prepare and serve lunch and then cleaned everything up. At 2:30 I read a story to the kids. I took a short break at 3:00 p.m. and then I took a group of children on a field trip to the park. We had one minor incident: Amy K. hit her head on the jungle gym. She has a small bump on her head, but she seems fine. I told her father about it when he picked her up. Finally, I helped check the children out as their parents arrived from 5:00 to 6:00 pm.

Alexander

D **Are the following statements true or false? Fill in the correct circle.**

	True	False
1. Alexander starts work in the afternoon.	○	○
2. Alexander was surprised by Ethan's behavior.	○	○
3. After they had lunch, they went to the park.	○	○
4. Alexander was worried about Amy's bump on the head.	○	○

E **Find the following words in Alexander's work journal and try to work out their meaning by using the context.**

sign in	check in	drop off	clean up	pick up	check

F Think about your job. (If you are a student or a homemaker, that is your job!) What did you do yesterday? Write your schedule below with the time that you did each thing.

Date:

G Use your list to write an entry in a journal.

H Show your journal to a partner. Ask your partner to help you correct any mistakes. Do you think it's useful to keep a journal? Discuss your answers.

Review

A **Use your dictionary to look up different word forms of vocabulary in this unit. Try to use the new word form in a sentence.**

EXAMPLE:

nouns: employee, employer

verb: ___to employ___

___Our company wants to employ people with good computer skills.___

1. noun: promotion

   verb: _____

   _____

2. verb: retire

   noun: _____

   _____

3. verb: commute

   noun (person): _____

   _____

4. noun: accomplishment

   verb: _____

   _____

B **Imagine you are an employer and need to hire several new employees. Use the vocabulary in the box to talk about the qualities you are looking for.**

friendly	courteous	funny	serious	demanding	respectful
strict	quiet	interesting	ambitious	hardworking	patient
relaxed	intelligent	easygoing	lazy	opinionated	reserved

EXAMPLE:

Student A: I think an ideal employee is hardworking.
Student B: I agree. Good employees shouldn't be lazy.

Review

C Circle the correct words in the sentences below.

1. Have you seen (my/mine) new pen?

2. (They/Their) cafeteria has delicious food, but (our/ours) is awful.

3. Can I use (your/yours) stapler? I can't find (my/mine.)

4. (Our/Ours) salary is low, but we get a lot of tips.

5. (My/Mine) benefits are really good, but (her/hers) are better.

D Complete the following sentences about work situations. Use the conditional with *might* or *could.*

1. If you don't mop the wet floor, _____.

2. The truck driver could get a ticket _____.

3. If those construction workers don't wear earplugs, _____.

4. If the gardener doesn't wear gloves, _____.

5. If your manager sees you leaving early, _____.

6. I might quit my job if _____.

E Work with a partner. Practice responding to compliments and criticism, using the sentences below.

EXAMPLE:
Student A: You look very professional today.
Student B: Thanks. It's nice of you to say so.

1. Your report was excellent!

2. I noticed you were late again today.

3. Can you be a little neater with your work?

4. You finished that project so quickly.

F With a partner, practice making and responding to polite requests in the following situations.

1. Ask your co-worker to let you use her computer.
2. Ask your employee to send a fax.
3. Ask your co-worker to help you lift a heavy box.
4. Ask your manager to give someone a message.

T E A M
P R O J E C T

Create an employee handbook

EMPLOYEE HANDBOOK
Table of Contents
Pay Stub Information 1
Benefits . . . .
Good Employee Behavior. . . . 4
Workplace Safety 6
Workplace Communication. . .11

With your team, you will create one section of an employee handbook. With your class, you will create a complete employee handbook.

1. Form a team with four or five students. Choose positions for each member of your team.

Position	Job Description	Student Name
Student 1 Leader	See that everyone speaks English. See that everyone participates.	
Student 2 Secretary	Write information for handbook.	
Student 3 Designer	Design handbook layout and add artwork.	
Students 4/5 Assistant(s)	Help secretary and designer with their work.	

2. With your class, decide what will be in your employee handbook. (Look at the Table of Contents above for ideas.) Decide what part of the handbook each team will create.

3. Create the text for your section of the employee handbook.

4. Create artwork for your section of the employee handbook.

5. As a class, create a table of contents and a cover. Put your handbook together.

6. Display your handbook so that other classes can see it.

PRONUNCIATION

Listen to the intonation of these polite requests and decide if the intonation is rising or falling. Mark the intonation with an arrow.

1. Could you give me a hand, please?

2. Would you mind looking over this report?

3. Would you come over here, please?

4. Can you help me?

LEARNER LOG

In this unit, you learned many things about being on the job. How comfortable do you feel doing each of the skills listed below? Rate your comfort level on a scale of 1 to 4.

1 = Not so comfortable **2** = Need more practice **3** = Comfortable **4** = Very comfortable

If you circle 1 or 2, write down the page number where you can review this skill.

Life Skill	Comfort Level				Page(s)
I can identify good employee behavior.	1	2	3	4	_____
I can talk about relationships at work.	1	2	3	4	_____
I can interpret a pay stub.	1	2	3	4	_____
I understand benefits.	1	2	3	4	_____
I can discuss workplace safety.	1	2	3	4	_____
I can respond to compliments and criticism.	1	2	3	4	_____
I can make and respond to polite requests.	1	2	3	4	_____
I can write a work journal.	1	2	3	4	_____

Grammar	Comfort Level				Page(s)
I can use possessive pronouns and possessive adjectives.	1	2	3	4	_____
I can use *might* and *could*.	1	2	3	4	_____

Academic Skill	Comfort Level				Page(s)
I can use my writing skills to write a work journal.	1	2	3	4	_____

Reflection

1. What was the most useful thing you learned in this unit? _____

_____

2. How will this help you in life? _____

_____

Citizens and Community

G O A L S

- Identify U.S. geographical locations
- Identify people and events in U.S. history
- Compare and contrast ideas

- Understand the system of U.S. government
- Use contrary-to-fact conditional statements
- Discuss community issues
- Express opinions

LESSON 1 ## The states of the United States

GOAL ▶ **Identify U.S. geographical locations** *Life skill*

A Look at the map of the United States. How many states are there? Write the names of the following cities in the spaces provided: Washington D.C.; Orlando; Philadelphia; New York; San Francisco; Los Angeles; Houston; Jamestown.

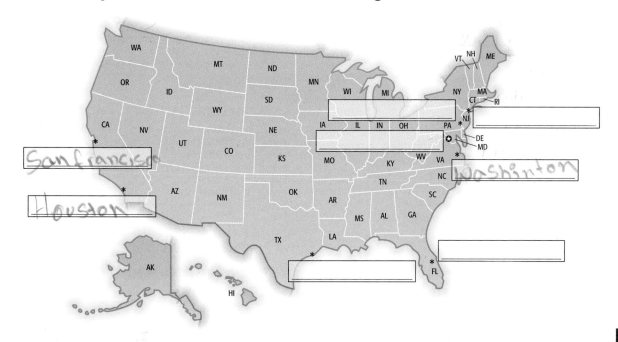

B Read the state abbreviations and then write the full state name. Ask a classmate or a teacher if you need help.

AL	Alabama	MT	Montana
AK	Alazka	NE	Nebraska
AZ	Arizona	NV	Nevada
AR	Arkansas	NH	New Hampshire
CA	California	NJ	New Jersey
CO	Colorado	NM	New Mexico
CT	Connecticut	NY	New Yor
DE	Delaware	NC	North Carolina
FL	Florida	ND	North Dakota
GA	Gorgia	OH	OHaio
HI	Haway	OK	Oklahoma
ID	Apaho	OR	Oregon
IL	Illinois	PA	Pensilvania
IN	Indiana	RI	Rhode Island
IA	A.	SC	Sur Carolina
KS	Kansas	SD	South Dakota
KY	Kentucky	TN	Tennessee
LA	Luisiana	TX	Texas
ME	Malme	UT	UTad
MD	Maryland	VT	Vermont.
MA	Mashachuselts	VA	Virginia
MI	Michigan	WA	Washington
MN	Minecota	WV	West Virginia
MS	Mississippi	WI	Wisconsin
MO	Missouri	WY	Wyoming

* Washington, D.C. is not a state.

C Ask your partner about the states he or she has visited. Which classmate has visited the most states?

D Look at the pictures of popular tourist attractions in the United States. What are they? Where are they located?

E Now listen to the lecture on important cities in the United States. As you listen, match the city on the right with the correct information on the left. Review the vocabulary with your teacher before you start.

Information	City
_h_ 1. The federal government is located here.	a. Houston, TX
_d_ 2. The Statue of Liberty is here.	b. Jamestown, VA
_g_ 3. A major port for the Pacific Ocean.	c. Hollywood, CA
_b_ 4. An English colony named after an English king.	d. New York, NY
_e_ 5. The Declaration of Independence was signed here.	e. Philadelphia, PA
_c_ 6. The film capital of the world.	f. Orlando, FL
_a_ 7. A major oil producer.	g. San Francisco, CA
_f_ 8. Disney World is located here.	h. Washington, D.C.

F What else do you know about the cities listed above?

G What are some other cities in the United States? What are they known for? Include your own city or the city nearest you.

_____

_____

American leaders and national holidays

GOAL ▶ Identify people and events in U.S. history   *Academic skill*

A What do you know about the famous American leaders pictured below?

Harriet Tubman

Abraham Lincoln

Franklin Delano Roosevelt

Martin Luther King, Jr.

 B Review the vocabulary below with your teacher. Then listen to descriptions of the people pictured above. Complete the sentences by writing the correct name.

1. _____**Abraham Lincoln**_____ wrote the Emancipation Proclamation.
2. _____Frankilin_____ was president during the Great Depression.
3. _____Frankiln_____ introduced the New Deal.
4. _____ worked on the underground railroad.
5. _____Abraham_____ was assassinated in 1865.
6. _____Abraham_____ was the 16th president of the United States.
7. _____Martin Luther____ gave a famous speech titled, "I Have a Dream."
8. _____Harriet Tub____ helped establish schools for freed slaves.
9. _____Martin Lurther____ was killed in 1968.
10. _____Herriet_____ and _____Martintin_____ were not presidents.

C George Washington's face is on the quarter and the one-dollar bill. Lincoln is on the penny and the five-dollar bill. What other famous Americans are pictured on U.S. currency? With a group, look at the currency you have with you now. What famous people can you identify?

D **Some American holidays honor famous people or historical events. Read about them below. Then answer the questions.**

Holiday	Date	Significance
Martin Luther King, Jr. Day	Third Monday in January	Dr. Martin Luther King, Jr. fought for civil rights and equal treatment for African Americans. His achievements are remembered on his birthday.
Presidents' Day	Third Monday in February	Americans once celebrated Washington's and Lincoln's birthdays in February. Now one day is dedicated to the memory of all former U.S. presidents.
Memorial Day	Last Monday in May	This day is to remember all the men and women who have died in war. Many people decorate soldiers' graves.
Independence Day	July 4th	On July 4th, 1776, the Declaration of Independence was signed. It said, "All men are created equal."
Labor Day	First Monday in September	This holiday honors all the workers in the United States.
Veterans' Day	November 11th	We celebrate this holiday to recognize all the men and women who fight or have fought for our country. Many soldiers and former soldiers march in parades.
Thanksgiving	Fourth Thursday in November	The Native Americans taught the Pilgrims, the first settlers from Europe, how to fish, hunt, and plant corn. On this day we remember the first Thanksgiving when the Pilgrims sat down for a feast with Native Americans, thanking God for their food and their new lives.

1. What do we celebrate on July 4th? _Independence day_
2. What holiday is in November? _Veteras Day and Thanksgiving_
3. Who attended the first Thanksgiving dinner? _Native America_
4. In what month do we remember presidents? _In February_
5. When do soldiers march in parades? _____ day memorial
6. When do we honor people who died fighting in wars? _to oner all workers_
7. What is the purpose of Labor Day? _Martin Luther king_
8. What holiday honors a civil rights leader? _____

E **Do you have similar holidays in your first country? Tell the class.**

F **Active Task:** What holidays are marked on the calendar? Go to the library or use the Internet to research what these holidays mean.

GOAL ▶ **Compare and contrast ideas** | **_Grammar_**

A The mayor is the top person in city government in most cities in the United States. Do you know who the mayor of your city is?

B Imagine that you are getting ready to vote for a new mayor of your city. Two candidates gave speeches about what is important to them. Read about their different points of view.

Kim Vo	Dawson Brooks
• build more parks	• drill for oil on empty land
• lower class size in elementary schools	• increase number of teachers per classroom
• lower the tuition for immigrant students	• raise the tuition for immigrant students
• spend tax dollars on wider sidewalks	• spend taxes to improve library facilities
• increase the number of police officers who patrol the streets	• spend money to retrain current police officers
• offer job training programs for homeless people	• offer incentives for individuals to start their own businesses

C **With a partner, compare the two candidates, using _but_ and _however._**

EXAMPLE:

Kim Vo wants to build more parks, _but_ Dawson Brooks wants to drill for oil on empty land.
Dawson Brooks wants to drill for oil on empty land; _however,_ Kim Vo wants to build more parks.

D **Write two sentences comparing Kim Vo and Dawson Brooks, using _but_ or _however._**

1. _____

_____

2. _____

_____

E **Which candidate would you vote for? Why? Write a paragraph on a separate sheet of paper.**

Ask students their feelings about the different topics listed below. Ask two students each question and fill in the chart. Ask: *How do you feel about . . . ?* Think of your own topic for the last question.

EXAMPLE:

Name	Topic	Agree	Disagree
Ex. *Enrico*	increasing the number of students in our class		✓
Ex. *Liz*		✓	

Name	Topic	Agree	Disagree
	building more schools in your community		

Name	Topic	Agree	Disagree
	bilingual education for children		

Name	Topic	Agree	Disagree
	(choose your own topic)_____		
	_____		

G **Study the chart with your teacher.**

Comparing and contrasting ideas

If two people share the same opinion, use *both . . . and* or *neither . . . nor.*

Both	Suzanna **and** Liz	<u>want</u> to increase the number of students in our class.
Neither	Enrico **nor** Ali	<u>wants</u> to increase the number of students in our class.

If two people don't share the same opinion, use *but* or *however.*

Enrico agrees with bilingual education,	**but** Liz doesn't.	Enrico agrees with bilingual education, but Liz doesn't.
Ali doesn't agree with bilingual education;	**however,** Suzanna does.	Ali doesn't agree with bilingual education; however, Suzanna does.

Punctuation note: Use a semicolon (;) before and a comma (,) after *however.*

H **On a separate sheet of paper, write sentences about the information you collected in exercise F.**

LESSON 4   U.S. government

| GOAL ▶ | Understand the system of U.S. government | *Academic skill* |

A Look at the diagram of the three branches that make up the United States government. What do you know about them?

Legislative   **Executive**   **Judicial**

B Read about the United States government. Then answer the questions after each section.

The United States Government

    The United States government has three branches—the Executive Branch, the Legislative Branch, and the Judicial Branch. It was set up this way so no one person would have too much power. With three branches, each branch balances out the other.

The Executive Branch

    In the Executive Branch are the president, the vice president, and the Cabinet. The president is the leader of the country and the Executive Branch. He can sign new laws, prepare the budget, and command the military. The vice president helps the president and is the leader of the Senate. Both the president and the vice president serve for four years and can be reelected only once. The Cabinet is a group of experts who advise the president. The president chooses his Cabinet members. They include the Secretary of State, the Secretary of Defense, and the Secretary of Education.

1. What does the president do? _____

2. What does the vice president do? _____

3. How long do the president and vice president serve? _____

4. What does the Cabinet do? _____

The Legislative Branch

The Legislative Branch, also known as the Congress, makes the laws for the United States. Congress has the power to declare war, collect taxes, borrow money, control immigration, set up a judicial and postal system, and the most important power, make laws.

This branch has the greatest connection to the people of the United States because this branch represents citizens. Congress has two parts, the House of Representatives and the Senate. The House of Representatives has 435 state representatives. Each state gets a certain number of representatives based on its population. They serve for two years and can be reelected. The Senate has 100 senators, two senators for each state. Senators serve for six years and can also be reelected.

1. What is another name for the Legislative Branch? _____

2. What does this branch do? _____

3. What are the two parts of this branch? _____

4. How many representatives are in the House? _____

5. What determines the number of representatives each state gets? _____

6. How long do representatives serve? _____

7. How many senators does each state have? _____

8. How long do senators serve? _____

The Judicial Branch

The third branch is the Judicial Branch, which includes the Supreme Court and the federal courts. The job of the courts is to interpret the laws made by the Legislative Branch. The Supreme Court is the highest court in the United States and has nine judges called justices. The justices listen to cases and make judgments based on the Constitution and the laws of the United States. The president and Congress choose the justices of the Supreme Court.

1. What is the role of the Judicial Branch? _____

2. What is the highest court in the United States? _____

3. How does a person become a judge on the Supreme Court? _____

_____

C Most cities have government officials who are elected to help run the city. Listen to the following people talk about their jobs, and fill in the chart with their duties.

Official	Duties
tax assessor	1. *helps set tax rates* 2. *decides on the value of property*
city clerk	1. 2.
city council member	1. 2.
superintendent of schools	1. 2.
mayor	1. 2.

D Discuss each of the above positions with a group. Which one would you most like to have? Why? Which one would you least like to have? Why?

E **Active Task:** Go to the library or use the Internet to find out who your local state representatives and senators are. Which parties do they belong to? Who is the governor of your state? Who is the mayor of your town?

> **GOAL** ▶ Use contrary-to-fact conditional statements   *Grammar*

A **Rosario's teacher asked her to write a paragraph about what she would do if she became president. Read what she wrote below.**

> If I won the presidential election, I would be the first female president. If I were president, nobody would be poor or homeless. I think if people had more money, they wouldn't commit crimes. In my opinion, we shouldn't spend so much money on the military. If scientists didn't have to build weapons, they would have more time to study other things. Maybe they would find a cure for cancer. I think I'd be a great president!

B **Read about contrary-to-fact conditional statements.**

Contrary-to-fact conditional statements						
if	**Subject**	**Past tense of verb**	**Subject**	***would***	**Base form of verb**	**Example sentence**
if	I, you, she, he, we, they	had / didn't have	I	would wouldn't	buy	If I had more money, I would buy a new house.
if	I, you, she, he, we, they	were / weren't	I	would wouldn't	spend	If I were president, I would spend more money on education.

Contrary-to-fact (or unreal) conditional statements are sentences that are not true and that the speaker thinks will probably never be true.

C **Fill in the sentences below with the correct form of the verb in parentheses.**

EXAMPLE:

I __*would give*__ (give) money to the homeless if I __*were*__ (be) president.

1. If people ___had___ (have) more money, they ___would be___ (be) happier.

2. If the president ___spent___ (spend) more on health, scientists ___discovered___ (discover) a cure for cancer.

3. If our classes ___were___ (be) larger, the teacher ___would___ (not have) much time for each student.

4. Maria ___would go___ (go) to medical school if she ___were___ (be) younger.

5. We ___would walk___ (walk) more, if we ___drove___ (drive) less.

D Write conditional statements, like the ones in exercise C, for each official listed on page 150. Then share your sentences with a partner.

EXAMPLE:
If I were the sheriff, I would hire more police officers.

1. _____

2. _____

3. _____

4. _____

5. _____

E What would you do if you were president? Talk about the things you would like to change.

Student A: What would you do if you were president?
Student B: Let's see. I think we need to improve our schools.
Student A: How would you do that?
Student B: I would pay teachers more. I would spend money on things like computers.

F Using the ideas you discussed above, write a paragraph about what you would do if you were president. Use Rosario's paragraph as an example. Then share your paragraph with the class. Who would the class elect to be president?

_____

_____

_____

_____

_____

_____

_____

GOAL ▶ Discuss community issues

A **Cherie lives in a small town in California. But it's not as nice as it used to be. Read about the problems in Cherie's community.**

    Hi, my name is Cherie. I live in a small community called Rosshaven in California. I moved here about ten years ago with my family because we wanted to live in a nice, safe community. But many things have happened in the past ten years.

    First of all, the neighborhood schools are overcrowded. Because our school system is so good, many families from outside neighborhoods send their kids to our schools. There are over 35 students in each classroom.

    Another problem is that there are many homeless people on our streets. It sometimes makes me nervous to have my kids walking home by themselves. I wish they could take a bus, but that's another problem. We don't have any public transportation here. When Rosshaven was first built, many wealthy people moved here. They all had cars, so there was no need for public transportation. But, now things have changed. I think it's time for me to go to a city council meeting to see what I can do for our community.

B **Cherie talks about three different problems in the paragraph above. List each one below.**

1. _Schools are overcrowded_
2. _Many homeless people on our streets_
3. _Poor_

C **With a group of students, discuss some possible solutions to each problem. Report your answers to the class.**

D Rosshaven is a nice place to live but, like every community, it has some problems. Match each problem with a possible solution. Then compare answers with a partner and say if you agree or disagree with each solution.

Problem	Solution: The city council should . . .
_C_ 1. Visitors park in resident parking spaces.	a. . . . set a curfew for teenagers.
_d_ 2. People don't clean up after their animals.	b. . . . raise taxes to help with recreation improvements.
_a_ 3. Teenagers are out late at night getting into trouble.	c. . . . give tickets to visitors who park in resident spaces.
_b_ 4. The parks are not well kept up.	d. . . . fine people who don't clean up after their pets.

E With a group, form a city council. Decide how you will solve the following problems and present your ideas to the class. The class will vote on which group would be the best city council.

1. There are no sidewalks on the busy streets in your town, and it is very dangerous. Many people get hurt because they walk too close to the cars. There is no space on the street to build sidewalks. What should we do to solve this problem?

2. The housing prices are going up in your community. It's difficult to find affordable rents and almost impossible to buy a house. Many people are moving away from the community to find cheaper housing. The community wants to maintain diversity, but only the very wealthy can afford to stay. What should we do about the housing costs?

3. The town's river was very dirty, but groups of citizens did a lot to clean it up. We want to increase taxes so we can build a new park along the river, but the growing town needs a new supermarket and more office space, too. Is there a way to make everyone happy?

F **Active Task:** Get a copy of the local paper. Find out what the current issues in your town are. Tell a classmate what you found out.

What's your opinion?

GOAL ▶ **Express opinions**

A **Study these expressions with your teacher.**

Expressing an opinion	
In my opinion, As I see it, Personally, I think . . .	I believe that . . . I think that . . . I feel that . . .

B **Write your opinion about the following topics, using the expressions above.**

EXAMPLE:

I believe that the president of the United States should be more concerned about the environment.

1. the president of the United States

_____

2. homework

_____

3. public transportation in my city

_____

4. learning English

_____

C **Practice the following expressions with your teacher.**

Asking about opinions
What do you think about . . . ? What's your opinion about . . . ? How do you feel about . . . ? I'd like to know your opinion about . . .

D **Ask a partner his or her opinion on the topics you wrote about above.**

EXAMPLE:

Student A: What's your opinion about homework?
Student B: I think that homework helps us learn English better.

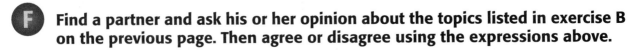

 E **Look at these expressions for agreeing and disagreeing.**

Agree	Disagree
I agree.	I disagree.
That's true!	I don't see it that way.
I couldn't agree more!	I don't think so.
That's exactly what I think.	I respect your opinion, but I think . . .
That's exactly how I feel.	I hate to disagree with you, but I believe . . .
You're right!	
That's my opinion, too.	

F **Find a partner and ask his or her opinion about the topics listed in exercise B on the previous page. Then agree or disagree using the expressions above.**

EXAMPLE:
Student A: What's your opinion about homework?
Student B: I think that homework helps us learn English better.
Student A: That's exactly what I think.

G **With a partner, discuss the following topics.**

1. Eliminating the death penalty
2. Raising the retirement age to 70
3. Raising the cost of gasoline so people will drive less
4. Smoking in public places
5. Raising the minimum wage
6. Building casinos in your town or city to raise money for schools

EXAMPLE:
Student A: What's your opinion about the death penalty?
Student B: I'm against the death penalty.
Student A: I disagree. I think we will have less crime if we have the death penalty.
Student B: I respect your opinion, but. . .

> If you agree with something, you are *for* it.
> If you disagree with something, you are *against* it.
> Examples: I am *for* the death penalty. I am *against* raising the cost of gasoline.

 H **Active Task:** Ask an American friend to give you his or her opinions on any of the subjects listed on this page.

Review

A **Improve your vocabulary. In this book, you have learned about ways to learn vocabulary and use a dictionary. Now put everything together and practice writing an entry to a vocabulary book.**

Word: ˈlegislature
Part of speech: noun
Definition: a branch of the U.S. government that passes laws
Related word(s): legislation (*n*), legislate (*v*)
Example sentence:
The <u>legislature</u> passed a new law on government taxes.

Start a vocabulary book of your own. Add any new words you learned inside or outside class. Start with a word or words from this unit.

federal	bilingual	assassinate	representative	civil rights

B **Write the full names of each state. See how many you can remember before you look back at page 142.**

1. NY _____
2. CA _____
3. WA _____
4. FL _____
5. TX _____

6. ME _____
7. IL _____
8. NV _____
9. HI _____
10. NJ _____

C **Remember what you learned about Harriet Tubman, Lincoln, Roosevelt, and Martin Luther King, Jr. Compare the leaders using *both/neither* and *but/however.* Your teacher can help you think of similarities and differences.**

EXAMPLES:
Neither Harriet Tubman nor Roosevelt was assassinated.
Both Harriet Tubman and Martin Luther King worked for civil rights.

_____

_____

_____

_____

Review

D Complete these contrary-to-fact conditionals with the correct form of the verb.

1. I _____ (work) faster if I _____ (have) a computer.

2. If she _____ (live) in Italy, she _____ (eat) pizza every day.

3. If it _____ (stop) raining, we _____ (play) outside.

4. If the town _____ (buy) more land, we _____ (build) schools.

5. I _____ (spend) more on education if I _____ (be) president.

6. If the president _____ (lower) taxes, he _____ (be) popular with Republicans.

7. People _____ (drive) less if gas _____ (be) more expensive.

8. If we _____ (prohibit) smoking in public places, everyone

    _____ (be) healthier.

E What would you do if you were mayor of your city? Write a paragraph stating your opinions about various local issues. Then say what you would do if you were mayor.

EXAMPLE:

In my opinion, the public transportation system in this town is very poor. The buses are always late because there is too much traffic. If I were mayor, I would build a subway system and . . .

_____

_____

_____

_____

_____

_____

_____

F Without looking at your paragraph, tell your partner about your ideas for the city. Ask for his or her opinions and express your agreement or disagreement.

T E A M
P R O J E C T

DEBATE
Date:
Is the death penalty
necessary ?
For
- It discourages
- It makes so
  safer.
- Prison
  overcrow

DEBATE
Date:
Is the death penalty
necessary ?
Against
- It is cruel.
- Mistakes can
  happen.
- Everyone deserves
  a second chance.

A debate

A debate is a formal discussion between two teams. Each team represents one point of view and argues for or against it. With a team, you will create a debate handout and then prepare a debate.

1. As a class, decide on two topics for your debate (see pages 146 and 156 for some ideas).

2. Form a team with four or five students. Choose positions for each member of your team.

Position	Job Description	Student Name
Student 1 Leader	See that everyone speaks English. See that everyone participates.	
Student 2 Secretary	Write information for the debate handout.	
Student 3 Debater	Debate the topic for your team.	
Students 4/5 Assistant(s)	Help secretary and debater with their work.	

3. As a class, assign two teams to each topic. Decide which team will be *for* the topic and which team will be *against* the topic.

4. With your team, research the topic and make a list of all the information you want to bring up in the debate.

5. Create your debate handout.

6. Prepare your debate.

7. Debate.

8. The rest of the class will vote on the team that presents the best argument.

PRONUNCIATION

Listen and mark the stressed word in each sentence.

1. Education is **very** important.
2. We need more schools.
3. I am against the death penalty.
4. Housing is not a serious issue.
5. We should have lower taxes.
6. We should spend more money on health.

LEARNER LOG

In this unit, you learned many things about citizens and community. How comfortable do you feel doing each of the skills listed below? Rate your comfort level on a scale of 1 to 4.

1 = Not so comfortable **2** = Need more practice **3** = Comfortable **4** = Very comfortable

If you circle 1 or 2, write down the page number where you can review this skill.

Life Skill	Comfort Level				Page(s)
I can identify geographical locations in the United States.	1	2	3	4	_____
I can talk about U.S. holidays.	1	2	3	4	_____
I can talk about the U.S. system of government.	1	2	3	4	_____
I can discuss community issues.	1	2	3	4	_____
I can express opinions.	1	2	3	4	_____
I can agree and disagree.	1	2	3	4	_____

Grammar

I can use *both, neither, but,* and *however* to compare and contrast ideas.	1	2	3	4	_____
I can use contrary-to-fact conditional statements.	1	2	3	4	_____

Academic Skill

I can read about the meaning of U.S. holidays.	1	2	3	4	_____
I can read about famous historical figures.	1	2	3	4	_____
I can read about the U.S. system of government.	1	2	3	4	_____

Reflection

1. What was the most useful thing you learned in this unit? _____

_____

2. How will this help you in life? _____

_____

Stand Out 3 Vocabulary List

Pre-Unit
Registration
date of birth P2
first name P2
last name P2
middle initial P2
occupation P2
Education
community college P6
elementary school P6
graduate P6
high school P6
junior high school P6
kindergarten P6
middle school P6
pre-school P6
technical college P6
vocational P6

Unit 1
Goals
achieve 3
apply 3
degree 3
educational 3
obstacle 5
occupational 3
personal 3
position 3
promote 3
solution 5
solve 5
Study habits
beneficial 8
concentrate 8
distractions 8
go over 8
harmful 8
improve 8
Family
cousin 10
co-worker 10
father-in-law 10
godfather 10
godmother 10
mother-in-law 10
partner 10
sibling 10
spouse 10
stepdaughter 10
stepson 10
Time management
accomplish 15
balance 15
check off 15

organized 15
schedule 15
task 15

Unit 2
Places
appliance store 21
bank 21
beauty salon 21
car wash 21
department store 21
gas station 21
grocery store 21
hardware store 21
hotel 21
jewelry store 21
laundromat 21
office supply store 21
ophthalmologist 21
pharmacy 21
post office 21
tailor 21
Money
account 23
bill 23
borrow 23
cash 23
coin 23
credit card 23
debit card 23
personal check 23
Computers
CD-ROM drive 27
CPU (central processing unit) 27
floppy drive 27
gigahertz 27
keyboard 27
megabytes 27
megahertz 27
memory 27
monitor 27
mouse 27
mouse pad 27
screen 27
speed 27
Adjectives
amazing 30
average 30
awesome 30
awful 30
delicious 30
horrible 30
incredible 30
mediocre 30
terrible 30

wonderful 30
Instructions and warnings
avoid 32
inhale 32
measure 32
rub 32
shake 32
spray 32
squeeze 32
swallow 32
wear 32
wet 32
wipe 32

Unit 3
Housing
air conditioning 43
apartment 42
balcony 43
carport 43
condominium 42
deposit 45
drip 50
electrician 50
exterminator 50
faucet 50
landlord 45
leak 53
lease 45
non-refundable 45
plumber 50
rental agreement 45
repairperson 50
restrictions 52
roaches 50
security guard 41
studio 42
tenant 45
utilities 45

Unit 4
Banks
ATM (automated teller machine) 63
direct deposit 63
minimum balance 63
service fee 63
teller 63
transaction 63
unlimited 63
Library
check out 65
circulating 65
fine 65
overdue 65
reference 65

renew 65
replacement 65
resources 65

Unit 5
Body parts
ankle 81
arteries 85
bones 85
brain 85
chest 81
chin 81
elbow 81
finger 81
heart 85
hip 81
intestines 85
joints 85
kidneys 85
knee 81
liver 85
lungs 85
muscles 85
neck 81
shoulder 81
stomach 81
toe 81
wrist 81
Doctors
allergist 82
cardiologist 82
dentist 82
dermatologist 82
gynecologist 82
obstetrician 82
ophthalmologist 82
pediatrician 82
podiatrist 82
psychiatrist 82
Illnesses
allergy 82
arthritis 85
asthma 82
blood pressure 85
cavity 82
depressed 82
diabetes 85
dizzy 82
fever 82
heart attack 85
pregnant 82
rash 82
seizure 85
stroke 85
ulcer 85
Nutrition
calcium 89

calories 89
carbohydrates 89
cholesterol 89
diabetic 89
diet 89
fiber 89
iron 89
protein 89
saturated fat 89
servings 89
sodium 89
vitamins 89
Physical fitness
aerobic 96
anxiety 96
build 96
cardiovascular 96
circulatory system 96
control 96
develop 96
endurance 96
flexibility 96
increase 96
lower 96
maintain 96
mood 96
muscular 96
promote 96
psychological 96
reduce 96
strength 96

Unit 6
Jobs
administrative assistant 102
auto technician 106
bookkeeper 101
clerk 106
computer programmer 102
custodian 106
dental hygienist 101
graphic artist 101
home health aide 101
landscaper 102
machine operator 102
manager 106
nanny 102
photographer 106
postal worker 102
receptionist 106
repair technician 102
Skills
answer 103
assemble 103
balance 103
calculate 105
cook 103

draw 103
drive 103
fix 103
operate 103
order 103
organize 105
pay attention to 105
repair 103
take care of 103
volunteer 103
Employment
attitude 106
benefits 106
experience 106
insurance 106
laid off 107
references 106
required 106
resume 106
salary 106
tools 106
training 106
Personality
arrogant 116
careful 116
cheerful 106
confident 116
enthusiasm 112
enthusiastic 116
friendly 116
funny 116
helpful 116
honest 116
intelligent 116
motivated 116
reliable 106
self-confidence 112
sensitive 116
sensitivity 112
sneaky 116
thoughtful 116
warm 116
warmth 112

Unit 7
Personality
ambitious 122
courteous 122
demanding 12
easygoing 122
hardworking 122
intelligent 122
interesting 122
lazy 122
opinionated 122
patient 122
quiet 122

Stand Out 3 Irregular Verb List

The following verbs are used in *Stand Out 3* and have irregular past tense forms.

base form	simple past	past participle	base form	simple past	past participle	base form	simple past	past participle
be	was, were	been	go	went	gone	run	ran	run
become	became	become	hang	hung	hanged/hung	say	said	said
break	broke	broken	have	had	had	sell	sold	sold
build	built	built	hear	heard	heard	shake	shook	shaken
buy	bought	bought	hold	held	held	show	showed	shown
catch	caught	caught	hurt	hurt	hurt	sit	sat	sat
choose	chose	chosen	keep	kept	kept	sleep	slept	slept
come	came	come	know	knew	known	speak	spoke	spoken
do	did	done	learn	learned	learned/learnt	spend	spent	spent
drink	drank	drunk	leave	left	left	stand	stood	stood
drive	drove	driven	lend	lent	lent	take	took	taken
eat	ate	eaten	lose	lost	lost	teach	taught	taught
fall	fell	fallen	make	made	made	tell	told	told
feel	felt	felt	mean	meant	meant	think	thought	thought
fly	flew	flown	meet	met	met	throw	threw	thrown
forget	forgot	forgotten	pay	paid	paid	wake	woke	woken
find	found	found	put	put	put	wear	wore	worn
get	got	gotten	read	read	read	win	won	won
give	gave	given	ride	rode	ridden	write	wrote	written

Grammar Reference

Frequency Adverbs

Sentence	Placement rule
Luisa *often* <u>goes</u> running.	Before the main verb
She <u>is</u> *usually* busy at weekends.	After the main verb *be*
Yes, <u>I</u> *always* <u>do</u>. / No, <u>he</u> *usually* <u>isn't</u>.	Between subject and verb in short answers

Note: *Rarely* and *never* are negative words. It is incorrect to use *not* and *never* in the same sentence.

Clauses with *because*

Sentence	Rule
My mother is very important to me *because* she taught me to be a good person.	When the *because* clause comes at the end of a sentence, no comma is needed.
Because my mother taught me to be a good person, she is very important to me.	When the *because* clause comes at the beginning of a sentence, use a comma.
My mother is very important to me *because* *she* taught me to be a good person.	Use a pronoun (e.g., *he, she, it, they*) to avoid repeating the subject noun.

To get something done

Subject	*get*	Object	Past participle	Sentence
I	get	my hair	cut	I get my hair cut every month.
she	got	her clothes	cleaned	She got her clothes cleaned yesterday.

Comparative Forms of Adjectives

	Adjective	Comparative	Rule	Sentence
Short adjectives	cheap	cheaper	Add –*er* to the end of the adjective.	Your computer was *cheaper* than my computer.
Long adjectives	expensive	more expensive	Add *more* before the adjective.	The new computer was *more expensive* than my old one.
Irregular adjectives	good bad	better worse	These adjectives are irregular.	The computer at school is *better* than this one.

Note: Remember to use *than* after a comparative adjective followed by a noun.

Superlative Forms of Adjectives

	Adjective	Superlative	Rule	Sentence
Short adjectives	cheap	the cheapest	Add –*est* to the end of the adjective.	Your computer is *the cheapest*.
Long adjectives	expensive	the most expensive	Add *most* before the adjective.	He bought *the most expensive* computer in the store.
Irregular adjectives	good bad	best worst	These adjectives are irregular.	The computers at school are *the best*.

Note: Always use *the* before a superlative adjective.

Comparatives Using Nouns

Our new apartment has *more bedrooms* than our old one. Our old apartment had *fewer bedrooms* than our new one.	Use *more* or *fewer* to compare count nouns.
Rachel's apartment gets *more light* than Pablo's apartment. Pablo's apartment gets *less light* than Rachel's apartment.	Use *more* or *less* to compare non-count nouns.

Superlatives Using Nouns

Rachel's apartment has *the most bedrooms*. Phuong's apartment has *the fewest bedrooms*.	Use *the most* or *the fewest* for count nouns.
Rachel's apartment has *the most light*. Phuong's apartment has *the least light*.	Use *the most* or *the least* for non-count nouns.

Grammar Reference

Adverbial clauses with *before, after, when*

Sentence	Rule
After I returned the books, I stopped by the bank to make a deposit.	The action closest to *after* happened first. (First, I returned the books. Second, I went to the bank.)
Before I went grocery shopping, I stopped by the cleaners.	The action closest to *before* happened second. (First, I went to the cleaners. Second, I went grocery shopping.)
When everyone left the house, I made my list of errands and went out.	The action closest to *when* is completed and then the next action begins. (First, everyone left. Second, I made my list and went out.)

Note: You can reverse the two clauses and the meaning stays the same.
Use a comma if the adverbial clause is first.

Present Perfect

Subject	*have*	Past participle		Length of time	Sentence
I, you, we, they	have	been	sick	since Tuesday	I *have been* sick since Tuesday.
she, he, it	has	had	a backache	for two weeks	She *has had* a backache for two weeks.

Note: Use the present perfect for events starting in the past and continuing up to the present.

Infinitives and Gerunds after Verbs

Verb	Infinitive or gerund	Example sentence	Verbs following the same pattern
want	takes an infinitive (*to* + verb)	He wants *to get* a job.	plan, decide
enjoy	takes a gerund (verb + *ing*)	He enjoys *fixing* bicycles.	finish, give up
like	takes either	He likes *to talk*. / He likes *talking*.	love, hate

Gerunds/Nouns after Prepositions

Subject	Verb	Adjective	Preposition	Gerund / Noun	Sentence
I	am	good	at	calculating	I am good at *calculating*.
she	is	good	at	math	She is good at *math*.

Note: Some other examples of adjectives + prepositions are: *interested in, afraid of, tired of, bad at, worried about.*

Would rather plus Verb

Subject	*would rather*	Base form	*than*	Base form	Sentence
I, you, she, he, it, we, they	would ('d) rather	work alone	than	work with people	I would rather work alone than work with people.

Note: You can omit the second verb if it is the same as the first verb.
EXAMPLE: *I would rather work nights than (work) days.*

Possessive Adjectives and Pronouns

		Sentence	Rule
Possessive adjectives	my, your, his, her, our, their	This is *her* office.	*Possessive adjectives* show possession of an object and come before noun.
Possessive pronouns	mine, yours, his, hers, ours, theirs	This office is *hers*.	Possessive pronouns *show possession of an object and act as a noun.*

Comparing and Contrasting Ideas

Both Enrico and Liz <u>want</u> to increase the number of students in our class. *Neither* Suzanna nor Ali <u>wants</u> to increase the number of students in our class.	If two people share the same opinion, use *both . . . and* (+ plural verb) or *neither . . . nor* (+ singular verb).
Enrico agrees with bilingual education, *but* Liz doesn't. Ali doesn't agree with bilingual education; *however,* Suzanna does.	If two people don't share the same opinion, use *but* or *however*.

Punctuation note: Use a semi-colon (;) before and a comma (,) after *however*.

Stand Out 3 Listening Scripts

Unit 1

p. 5, Lesson 3, exercise B

Speaker 1: My name is Tuba Kambriz. I came here from Afghanistan five years ago. My husband had to come here for business, so my whole family moved here. Right now, we don't have enough money to pay the bills, so my goal is to get a job to help my husband with money. But I have an obstacle—time. It will be difficult to work because I have to take care of the children and the house. One solution is to work part-time while my children are in school. Another solution is to have my mother help out around the house and help take care of the children. If we all work together, we will achieve our goal.

Speaker 2: I'm Lam, and I came to the United States from Vietnam many years ago. I was a political prisoner during the Vietnam War, and now I'm happy to be safe in America with my family. The most important people in my life are my grandchildren. My goal is to send my grandchildren to college. But there is an obstacle. We don't have enough money to send them to college. I want them to have the education I never did, so I think it's very important for them to go to school. My wife thought of one solution. She suggested they apply for scholarships. This is a good idea because both girls are very smart. The girls came up with another solution. They said they could work part-time while going to school. We have been saving every penny we can to help them. I hope everything works out in the end.

p. 10, Lesson 5, exercise A

Luisa: Here are some pictures of my wedding day. Weddings are amazing because all of the important people in your life come together on one day. This is a picture of me with my new family. The handsome man is my husband, of course! These are his parents—my mother-in-law and my father-in-law. They are really wonderful people. The woman in the pink dress is my husband's sister, Juliet. Here's another picture of two special people who are important for a lot of reasons. This is Aunt Rosa. Rosa is my mother's sister. She is my godmother as well, so we have a close relationship. As a godmother, she had a special part in the wedding. That's her daughter Isabella. My cousin Isabella and I are almost the same age. She is a good friend to me. I got her a job at the restaurant I work at. Now, we are cousins, friends, and co-workers, too.

p. 15, Lesson 7, exercise B

Time management is important for several reasons. First of all, it helps you stay organized. Second of all, you can make sure you are accomplishing everything that needs to get done. And third, you can make time for family and friends and things that matter most. One of the best ways to manage your time is to keep a schedule. First, write down everything you need to do in a week. This includes work, school, children, and other tasks. Then put each of these into a time slot. Of course, follow your schedule. And most important, check things off once they have been completed. There are some easy ways to add more time to your day. One, wake up a few minutes earlier. Even ten or fifteen minutes will give you some extra time to study or do things around the house. Two, have your family or friends help you with things you need to get done. For example, having your children help you with the housework will help you finish twice as fast. Three, try doing two tasks at once. Instead of just eating lunch, eat lunch and review your verb tenses. We call this killing two birds with one stone! There are some other important things to consider about time management. First of all, remember the important people in your life. Did you put time in your schedule to visit them, write them a letter, or even call them? Also remember your values. If you value exercise, you must schedule time to exercise. And finally, you are the boss of your schedule. Don't let your schedule control you. Managing your time will give you several benefits in life. You will find that you have more free time. In addition, you will feel less stressed because you are more organized. Also, you will have time to see the people in your life who matter most. And lastly, you will feel better about yourself.

Unit 2

p. 30, Lesson 5, exercise A

Ex. Janie: I was at the mall yesterday and I saw the cutest shoes! But when I tried them on, they were so uncomfortable! Some people will give up comfort for fashion, but not me!

1. Thomas: My wife and I went to an electronics store last week to look at computers for our kids. We were really surprised at how reasonable they were. We'll have enough money to buy one for each of them.

2. Rosa: Do you believe those car salesmen? They are so pushy and they won't leave you alone! The next time I buy a car I'm going to look in the paper for a private owner.

3. Nicolai: Man, those televisions are cheap! At those prices, I could buy one for each room in the house. But I'd better not. My wife would kill me if I came home with six new televisions.

4. Yen: A tip? You want me to leave a tip for that horrible service? The waitress never asked us if we wanted anything to drink, the food took an hour to get here and then it was cold, and on top of that, it took her twenty minutes to bring the check. She doesn't deserve a tip!

Unit 3

p. 43, Lesson 2, exercise B

Maryanne: I think it's time to move. This apartment is too small.

Vu: I'm making more money now. I think we can afford a bigger place.

Truyen: All right! Now I can have my own room.

Maryanne: Not so fast. We are not that rich. But it is hard with all four of you sharing one room. We need one bedroom for the girls and one for the boys.

Vu: Yes. A three-bedroom would be perfect.

Truyen: I want two bathrooms. Nga and Truc take hours to do their hair!

Maryanne: We don't have air conditioning. I want air conditioning in the new place.

Vu: Air conditioning would be really nice. It gets so hot in the summer.

Truyen: Can we get a pool too?

Vu: Well, we don't really need a pool. (Pause) Well, let's try to find a place that has one.

Truyen: Don't forget we need a yard for the dog. We don't have one now.

Maryanne: Of course, we want a nice space for Fluffy.

Vu: Let's get the paper and start looking for a place today!

p. 55, Lesson 7, exercise A

Maryanne: Now that you are making more money, I think we need to make a new budget.

Vu: OK, let's talk about income first. With the raise, my income will be $3,000 a month.

Maryanne: Great! And with my part-time job, I'm still making about $1000 a month.

Vu: OK, that's it for income. The rent for our new apartment is going to be $1350 a month. It's a bigger place, so our utilities are going to go up.

Maryanne: Yeah, I was thinking our gas bill will probably be around $40 a month and our electricity will be about $60. Especially with that air conditioning.

Vu: That sounds about right. What about the phone, cable, and Internet?

Maryanne: Well, if we use the same companies, they'll be the same.

Vu: Is the phone bill really $65 a month?

Maryanne: Yes, it's an average. It includes long-distance calls to your mom in Vietnam.

Vu: I see. How much do you spend on groceries each month?

Maryanne: About $450. That shouldn't change. Um, what do we spend on the car?

Vu: Good news. We paid off the loan last month. Now the only expense is gas and maintenance.

Maryanne: Right. Let's budget $150 for that.

Vu: OK, well, it looks like we've got some extra money. Let's talk about how we can use it.

Unit 4

p. 61, Lesson 1, exercise A

Gloria is new to the community. First of all, she needs to open a checking account at her local bank so she can pay her bills. Second, she needs to go the Department of Motor Vehicles to register her car and renew her driver's license. For now, she will need to use public transportation. But she doesn't know where to get a bus

schedule. She'll have to ask at the bus station. Also, she would like to take some ESL classes to improve her English. There is a community college nearby; maybe she could try there. Her children would like to play sports so she needs to find a place for them to do that. Perhaps she can call the Department of Parks and Recreation. Also, the kids want to use computers to e-mail their friends from the old neighborhood. They'll probably have the Internet at the public library.

Unit 5

p. 89, Lesson 5, exercises B and C

Part 1:

Grandma: Darla, I need your help.

Darla: Sure what can I do, Grandma?

Grandma: Well, my doctor says I need to pay attention to nutrition. But I can't understand the nutrition label.

Darla: Oh sure, I can help. Let's look at this box of macaroni and cheese. What's your first question?

Grandma: Well, I have high blood pressure. I shouldn't have a lot of salt. I don't see salt on this label.

Darla: Oh, you need to look at sodium. Sodium amount tells you how much salt there is.

Grandma: So there is 470 mg of sodium in this box?

Darla: No, the amount they give you is the amount in each serving.

Grandma: How do I know how much a serving is?

Darla: They tell you on the label. See the serving size?

Grandma: Okay. I see there are two servings in this box, one for me and one for Grandpa.

Darla: What's next?

Grandma: I need to watch calories if I want to lose weight. How many calories should I have each day?

Darla: About 2000. You can have more calories if you are active.

Part 2:

Grandma: What should I eat if I want to have a healthy heart?

Darla: Oh, you should avoid cholesterol and saturated fat.

Grandma: Okay, Grandpa is a diabetic. He needs to limit sugar.

Darla: Yes, sugar is on the nutrition label.

Grandma: Now, Grandpa and I both need something to help digestion.

Darla: You need a lot of fiber.

Grandma: One last question. Why do older women need to have a lot of calcium?

Darla: Oh, that's because women need calcium to protect against bone disease.

Grandma: That's really helpful. Thanks, Darla.

Unit 6

p. 109, Lesson 4, exercise E

Rules for Filling Out an Application

1. Use a <u>dark pen</u>—blue or <u>black</u> ink.
2. Don't <u>cross out</u> any mistakes. Use correction fluid to <u>correct</u> any mistakes.

3. Answer every <u>question</u>. If the question doesn't apply to you, put <u>NA</u> (not applicable).
4. Tell the <u>truth</u>! Never <u>lie</u> on your job application.
5. Don't <u>bend</u> or wrinkle the application.
6. Keep the application <u>clean</u>—no food or coffee stains!
7. Write as <u>neatly</u> as possible. <u>Type</u> it if you can.
8. If you don't <u>understand</u> the question, ask someone before you answer it.

p. 120, Pronunciation
1. I'm really interested in this job. (enthusiastic)
2. I'm quite good at using computers. (bored)
3. I enjoy working on a team. (confident)
4. I like to discuss ideas with other people. (kind)
5. I want to use my skills and experience. (impatient)
6. I want to get a job with more responsibility. (friendly)

Unit 7
p. 121, Lesson 1, exercise A
Leticia: Hi. I'm Leticia. I work for New Wave Graphics as an administrative assistant. I really like my job. I come on time to work every day, and I never leave early. I try to keep my workspace very clean, and I never eat at my desk. When my manager asks me to do something, I get it done as soon as I can. I obey all the company policies, especially the safety rules. I try to be friendly to everyone I work with, even when I'm having a bad day. I am constantly learning new computer skills so I can be ready to move up the ladder when a position becomes available. New Wave Graphics is a great company to work for and I hope to stay here a long time.

So: Hey, I'm So. I stock shelves at Johnson's Market. I'm supposed to come in at twelve and leave at eight but I figure as long as I get my work done, it doesn't matter what time I get there. I like to wear casual clothes and my manager always tells me to dress more neatly but he's never around anyway, so I usually don't bother. The best part about this job is all the food. I stock the shelves with all the dry goods, such as cereal, crackers, and pasta. And there's always some extra stuff that doesn't fit on the shelves, so I usually take a few things home with me. I figure they should be paying me more for all the work I do, so I take a few things home to make up for it. I don't really like the guys I work with. They try too hard to impress the manager so that they can get raises. I try to stay away from them and just get my work done as fast as I can. It's an OK job. I'll find something better soon.

p. 127, Lesson 4, exercise B
Career Counselor: Hello, future employees. My name is Kevin Daly and today's workshop is on company benefits. Can someone tell me what benefits are?
Participant: That's when the company pays for you to go to the doctor.
Career Counselor: Yes, that's true, but companies offer more than just health benefits. To give you an example of the different types of benefits that companies offer their employees, I'm going to talk about three different companies.

The first one is Set It Up Technology. This company helps small businesses set up computers in their offices. Their employees work six days a week, but they are paid a good salary. All employees are given full medical and dental insurance. In addition, employees are given twelve sick days and two weeks vacation a year. But the best benefit this company offers is its 401K retirement account. The company will match every dollar an employee contributes to the account.

The second company I'd like to talk about is Machine Works, an assembly plant that makes sewing machines. This company offers its full-time employees health benefits. There is no dental insurance. Machine Works gives their employees one week of sick leave and one week vacation. This company pays a generous amount of overtime, but there is no 401K offered by Machine Works.

The final company I'm going to talk about is Lino's Ristorante. This is a big chain restaurant so their benefits are pretty good. Employees receive health insurance but no dental benefits. Full-time employees receive eight sick days a year. All employees are given one week of paid vacation time every year. Lino's offers a 401K plan and they will contribute 50 cents for every dollar that you contribute.

So these are some examples of benefits that different companies offer. Are there any questions?

p. 132, Lesson 6, exercise B
1.
Speaker 1: That was an excellent presentation!
Speaker 2: Thanks, I'm glad to hear it.
2.
Speaker 1: You need to work a little faster.
Speaker 2: I'm sorry. I'll try to do better next time.
3.
Speaker 1: You are a talented salesperson.
Speaker 2: It's nice of you to say so.
4.
Speaker 1: You shouldn't wear that shirt to work.
Speaker 2: I'm sorry. I won't wear it again.
5.
Speaker 1: You are one of our best workers.
Speaker 2: Thank you. I appreciate you telling me that.
6.
Speaker 1: Please don't take such long breaks.
Speaker 2: OK. It won't happen again.

p. 133, Lesson 6, exercise E
1. Bob, would you mind coming to my office for a minute?
2. Give me that hammer.
3. Hey. We need more coffee.
4. Would you mail this package, please?

p. 143, Lesson 1, exercise E

Now that we've talked about various states in the United States, I'd like to tell you about a few of the most important cities. I'll start with one that really isn't called a city but it's definitely very important—Washington, D.C. The D.C. stands for District of Columbia, which is what it is, a district. This is where the federal government is located: the White House, the Capitol building, and the Supreme Court.

Historically, two of the most important cities are Jamestown and Philadelphia. When the settlers first came from England in the 1600s, they came to Jamestown, Virginia and named this first colony after King James of England. Many years later, the representatives of the thirteen colonies declared themselves an independent nation and wrote the Declaration of Independence in Philadelphia, which was the same place the Constitution was written. Also on the East Coast, New York City was established and this is where European immigrants first came. They came to an island off the coast of New York, Ellis Island, home of the Statue of Liberty, given to the United States by France in 1886.

Other famous cities include San Francisco, Los Angeles, and Houston. San Francisco, where the famous Golden Gate Bridge is located, was one of the first established cities in California because it was a port for ships coming in from the Pacific Ocean. Hollywood made Los Angeles the film capital of the world in the mid 1900s and has grown ever since. And finally, Houston, Texas put itself on the map by being one of the largest oil producers in the United States. And who could forget Mickey Mouse, Donald Duck, and the whole Disney gang? Yes, Disneyland is in California, but Disney World is located in Orlando, Florida.

These are some of the most popular cities in the United States. Can you think of some other popular cities?

p. 144, Lesson 2, exercise B

Abraham Lincoln was elected in 1861 as the 16th president of the United States. At the time, the United States was in a civil war because the North and the South were divided on the issue of slavery. Lincoln wanted the nation to stay united, but he was against slavery. On January 1, 1863, he signed a document called the Emancipation Proclamation, which freed all slaves. Two years later, he was killed. Today we remember Lincoln by celebrating his birthday on February 12.

Born a slave in 1820 on the eastern shore of Maryland, **Harriet Tubman** fled north to freedom. There she joined the secret network of free blacks and white sympathizers who helped runaways—the 'underground railroad.' She became a 'conductor' who risked her life to lead her people to freedom. She kept returning to Maryland to bring her relatives and as many as 300 other slaves north. When the Civil War began, she worked among the slaves who fled their masters and joined Union lines. After the war she cared for orphaned and invalid blacks. She also worked to establish freedmen's schools in the South.

Franklin Delano Roosevelt was president from 1932 to 1945. When he was president, the United States was in a great depression, meaning that the country was having very serious economic problems. Many people were unemployed and homeless. People demanded help from the government and Roosevelt offered a solution he called the New Deal. The New Deal created jobs, helped businesses get loans, and pulled the country out of the Depression.

Dr. Martin Luther King, Jr. was a civil rights leader who fought for equal treatment of African Americans. He believed all human beings have the same rights. His famous speech, "I Have a Dream" includes the famous line, "I have a dream that my four little children will one day live in a nation where they will not be judged by the color of their skin, but by the content of their character." Americans were shocked when he was killed in 1968. Today we remember Martin Luther King, Jr. by celebrating his birthday on the third Monday in January.

p. 150, Lesson 4, exercise C

1. Hi, my name is Jim and I'm the tax assessor. I help set tax rates by deciding the value of property. Some people don't like me because they think I cause higher taxes. But I'm just doing my job.

2. Hello there, I'm Su Young. I'm the city clerk. As city clerk, I keep track of records of property, local businesses, and registered voters. I also issue birth certificates and marriage licenses. So if you're going to get married or have a baby, come see me!

3. I'm Christopher Erikson, a city council member. I help to represent this community. All the council members meet with the mayor to discuss and solve community problems. It's really important to help make our community a better place to live.

4. Hi, my name is Sheryl and I'm the superintendent of schools. I oversee the county schools and I help them do their job to provide a good education to our children. It's a very important job!

5. My name is Matt Peterson and I'm the mayor of this town. I'm the head of the city government and I work with all the city council members to keep our community strong and happy.

Stand Out 3 Skills Index

ACADEMIC SKILLS

Grammar

Adjectives, 30–31, 105, 118, 122
    Comparative and superlative, 27–29, 37, 38, 164
    Positive and negative, 31
    Possessive, 123
Adverbs
    Of frequency, 3, 164
    Time clauses, 73–74, 78
    while, 51
Agreement/disagreement, expressions of, 156
Clauses
    Adverbial, 73–74, 78, 165
    With *because*, 11–12, 13, 18, 164
Comparatives and superlatives, 27–29, 37, 38, 42, 58
Comparison
    both/neither in, 157, 165
    but/however in, 146, 147, 157
Nouns
    Count and noncount, 42, 164
    After prepositions, 165
Prepositions, 105, 165
Pronouns, possessive, 123–124, 138
Sentences, compound and complex, 51
Sequencing transitions, 35–36, 37, 38, 75, 76
Verbs, 32
    Conditionals, 130, 138, 151–152, 158, 87–88, 98
    Future tense, 3–4, 87–88, 98
    Gerunds, 104, 117, 165
    to get something done, 164
    Imperatives, 33–34, 36, 37, 165
    Infinitives, 104, 105, 117
    Irregular, 163
    Modals, 130
    Past continuous tense, 58
    Past participles, 83
    Present continuous tense, 51
    Present perfect tense, 83–84, 98, 165
    Present tense, 2, 3, 87
    Simple past tense, 58
    would rather, 115, 118, 165

Graphs, Tables, Charts, and Maps

1, 9, 14, 15, 16, 22, 27, 28, 29, 31, 33, 56, 63–64, 66–67, 70–72, 74, 82, 84, 87, 104, 115, 123, 133, 147, 150, 172

Listening

Conversations, 48, 49, 55, 89, 112, 121, 133
Lectures, 143
Questions, 61
Statements, 5, 109, 127, 132
Vocabulary, 144

Mathematics

Calculations using charts, 66–67
Tax calculations, 126

Pronunciation

Intonation, 40, 120, 140
Stressed words, 60, 80, 100, 117, 160
Syllables, 20

Reading

Abbreviations, 41, 57, 106, 142, 157
Advertisements, 25–26, 41–42, 57, 106–107
Articles, 94
Bills, 47
Comprehension, 43, 46, 56, 107, 135, 148, 149
Conversations, P3, 30, 83, 108, 130
Directions and instructions, 78
Graphs, tables, maps and charts, 1, 11, 15, 22, 27, 28, 29, 33, 44, 56, 63–64, 66–67, 70–72, 74, 84, 87, 104, 115, 123, 133, 147, 172
Idiomatic expressions, 22
Letters, 110–111
Outlines, 15
Paragraphs, 5, 6, 8, 35, 36, 43, 51, 52, 73, 75, 96, 110
Pay stubs, 125
Predictions, 94
Product labels, 32–34, 89–90
Rental agreements, 45–46
Statements, 13, 64, 92, 148, 149
Stories, 3, 153
Telephone directories, 68–69
Vocabulary, P6, 16, 21, 25, 27, 30, 37, 57, 63, 65, 71, 77, 81, 97, 135, 161–163
Work journals, 135

Speaking

Conversation, P3, P4, 2, 4, 48, 49, 50, 61, 69, 77, 85, 97, 102, 105, 122, 132–133, 138
Discussion, 92, 93, 96, 108, 112, 126, 136, 150, 153, 154, 156, 158, 159
Interviewing, 116, 118
Questions
    Answering, 46, 52, 89, 92, 122
    Asking, 1–2, 14, 44, 46, 62, 63, 70, 90, 147, 155, 156
Stories, 93
Vocabulary, 63, 125

Writing

Advertisements, 39
Brochures, 79
Charts, tables, maps and charts, 4, 9, 14, 16, 18, 22, 31, 82, 127, 147, 150
Conversations, 69, 83
Directions and instructions, 34, 36, 78
Employee handbook, 139
Forms, P2, 24, 109
Graphs, tables, maps and charts, 78
Journal entries, 136
Letters, 53, 54, 110–111
Lists, 37, 65, 136
Medical history forms, 85–86
Paragraphs, P5, 35, 36, 38, 64, 75–76, 146, 151, 152, 158
Plans, 99
Product labels, 39
Questions, P2, 46, 62, 118
Registration forms, 24
Responses to questions, 96, 111, 114–115
Sentences, 2, 9, 11, 14, 17, 18, 28, 29, 34, 38, 42, 74, 84, 98, 105, 115, 124, 131, 155
    Conclusion sentences, 6, 75
    Support sentences, 6, 75
    Topic sentences, 6, 75
Statements, 88, 152
Vocabulary, 9, 10, 101, 137, 157, 161–163

LEARNER LOGS

20, 40, 60, 80, 100, 120, 140, 160

LIFE SKILLS

Consumer Education

Advertisements, 25–26, 41–42
Household repairs, 50, 53–54
Housing choices, 41–44, 59
Product labels, 32–34, 39
Rental agreements, 45–46
Tenants and landlords, 52–54
Utilities, 47–49, 58

Family and Parenting

Family relationships, 10

Government and Community Resources

Business services, 21–22, 30–31, 61, 69

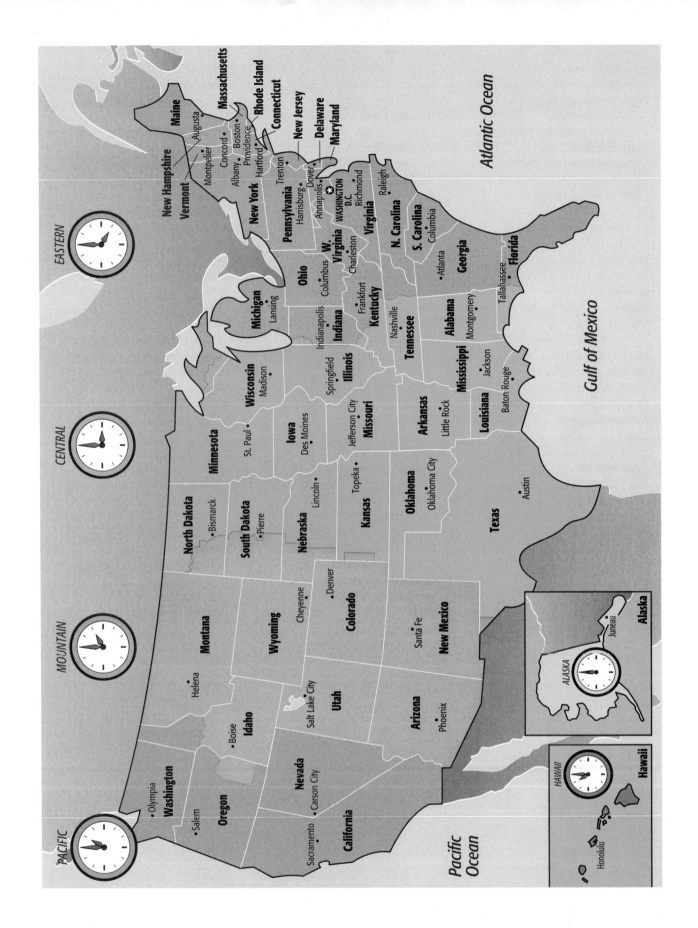

Atlantic Ocean

Gulf of Mexico

Pacific Ocean

EASTERN

CENTRAL

MOUNTAIN

PACIFIC

ALASKA

HAWAII

Maine
Augusta

New Hampshire
Vermont
Montpelier
Concord
Albany
Boston
Providence
Hartford
Trenton

Massachusetts
Rhode Island
Connecticut
New Jersey
Delaware
Maryland

New York
Pennsylvania
Harrisburg
Dover
Annapolis
WASHINGTON D.C.
Richmond
Raleigh

W. Virginia
Charleston
Virginia
N. Carolina
S. Carolina
Columbia

Ohio
Columbus
Frankfort
Kentucky
Nashville

Atlanta
Georgia
Tallahassee
Florida

Michigan
Lansing

Indianapolis
Indiana
Illinois
Springfield

Tennessee
Alabama
Montgomery

Wisconsin
Madison

Iowa
Des Moines

Missouri
Jefferson City

Mississippi
Jackson

Minnesota
St. Paul

Topeka
Kansas

Arkansas
Little Rock

Louisiana
Baton Rouge

North Dakota
Bismarck

South Dakota
Pierre

Nebraska
Lincoln

Oklahoma
Oklahoma City

Montana
Helena

Wyoming
Cheyenne

Denver
Colorado

Santa Fe
New Mexico

Texas
Austin

Idaho
Boise

Salt Lake City
Utah

Arizona
Phoenix

Nevada
Carson City

Olympia
Washington
Salem
Oregon

Sacramento
California

Alaska
Juneau

Hawaii
Honolulu